Birds of Virginia

Todd Telander

FALCONGUIDES

GUILFORD, CONNECTICUT
HELENA, MONTANA
AN IMPRINT OF GLOBE PEQUOT PRESS

To my wife, Kirsten, my children, Miles and Oliver, and my parents,
all of whom have supported and encouraged me through the years.
Special thanks to Mike Denny for his expert critique of the illustrations.

To buy books in quantity for corporate use
or incentives, call **(800) 962-0973**
or e-mail **premiums@GlobePequot.com**.

FSC
www.fsc.org
MIX
Paper from
responsible sources
FSC® C005010

FALCONGUIDES®

FalconGuides is an imprint of Globe Pequot Press.
Falcon Field Guides is a trademark and Falcon, FalconGuides, and Outfit
Your Mind are registered trademarks of Morris Book Publishing, LLC.

Illustrations: Todd Telander
Project editor: David Legere
Text design: Sheryl P. Kober
Layout: Sue Murray

Library of Congress Cataloging-in-Publication Data is available on file.

ISBN 978-0-7627-7893-5

Printed in the United States of America

10 9 8 7 6 5 4 3 2 1

Contents

Passerines

Introduction

Virginia is made up of three distinct geographic zones. The east is dominated by the high mountains of the Blue Ridge and its adjoining valleys and is densely forested. Many eastern Warblers breed in this area, and it is home to the Ruffed Grouse and Common Raven. The mountains slope eastward to rolling country known as the highlands or the Peidmont Plateau, which includes mixed woodlands, pastures, and rich river systems. Farther west beyond the Fall Line is the Coastal Plain, a flat region of sandy soil, mostly coniferous forests, marshes, and coastal shoreline that meets with the vast Chesapeake Bay and Atlantic Ocean. Here you will find all manner of shorebirds, herons, gulls, terns, and waterfowl. This geographic diversity, with its accompanying array of climatic and vegetative zones, provides for an incredible number and variety of bird species. Virginia supports habitat for resident breeders and seasonal visitors, as well as those birds passing through on migration to and from South America and Canada. Although Virginia is home to or visited by over 340 species of birds, this guide describes some of the most common birds you are likely to encounter, and it will give you a good start to understanding the birdlife here.

Notes about the Species Accounts

Order

The order of species listed in this guide is based on the latest version of the *Check-List of North American Birds,* published by the American Ornithologist's Union. The arrangement of some groups, especially within the nonpasserines, may be slightly different from that of older field guides, but in an effort to remain current, I have used the most recent arrangement here.

Names

Both the common name and the scientific name are included for each entry. Because common names tend to vary regionally, or there may be more than one common name for each species, the universally accepted scientific name of genus and species (such as *Hylocichla mustelina* for the Wood Thrush) is more reliable to be certain of identification. Also, one can often learn interesting facts about a bird by the English translation of its Latin name. For example, *hylocichla* refers to "forest," its favored habitat, and *mustelina* refers to the weasel-like color of the plumage.

Families

Birds are grouped into families based on similar traits and genetics. When trying to identify an unfamiliar bird, it often can be helpful to first place it into a family, which will reduce your search to a smaller group. For example, if you see a long-legged, long-billed bird lurking in the shallows, you can begin by looking in the family group of Ardeidae (Herons, Egrets) and narrow your search from there.

Size

The size given for each bird is the average length, from the tip of the bill to the end of the tail if the bird was laid out flat. Sometimes females and males vary in size, and this variation is described in the text. Size can be misleading if you are looking at a small bird that happens to have a very long tail or bill. It can be more effective to judge the bird's relative size by comparing the size differences between two or more species.

Season

The season given in the accounts is the time when the greatest number of individual birds occurs in Virginia. Some species are year-round residents that breed here. Others may spend only summers or winters here, and some may be transient, only stopping during the spring or fall during migration. Even if only part of the year is indicated for a species, be aware that there may be individuals that arrive earlier or remain for longer than the given time frame. Plumage also changes with the season for many birds, and this is indicated in the text and illustrations.

Habitat

A bird's habitat is one of the first clues to its identification. Note the environment where you see a bird and compare it with the description listed. This can be especially helpful when identifying a bird that shares traits with related species. For example, Cattle Egrets and Snowy Egrets are similar in appearance, but Cattle Egrets are found in drier fields and pastures, while Snowy Egrets prefer swamps and open water.

Illustrations

The illustrations show the adult bird in the plumage most likely to be encountered during the season(s) it is in Virginia. If it is likely that you will find more than one plumage during this time, the alternate plumage is also shown. For birds that are sexually dimorphic (females and males look different), illustrations of both sexes are usually included. Other plumages, such as those of juveniles and alternate morphs, are described in the text.

Bird Topography and Terms

Bird topography describes the outer surface of a bird and how various anatomical structures fit together. Below is a diagram outlining the terms most commonly used to describe the feathers and bare parts of a bird.

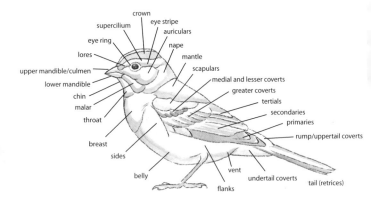

NONPASSERINES

Brant, *Branta bernicla*
Family Anatidae (Geese, Ducks, Mergansers)
Size: 25.5"
Season: Winter
Habitat: Coastal bays and marshes or nearby fields

The Brant is a small, dark, fairly short-necked goose with a short, stubby bill. Its plumage is barred sooty gray above with black flight feathers. Its underparts are a mix of gray and white down to the flanks, then pure white to the short, black-edged tail. The head and neck are black with a thin, streaked white partial neck band (lacking in juveniles). The sexes are similar, and Pacific races tend to be darker along the breast and sides. The Brant feeds in the water for eelgrass and aquatic invertbrates, or in nearby fields for insects, and emit a low, throaty, croaking call. Brant fly low to the ground in rather loose, unorganized groups. The adult eastern morph is illustrated.

Snow Goose, *Chen caerulescens*
Family Anatidae (Geese, Ducks,
Mergansers)
Size: 28"
Season: Winter
Habitat: Grasslands, marshes

The Snow Goose forms huge, impressive flocks when it visits
Virginia during the winter. It has two color forms: the "blue" and
the more common "white." The white form is predominantly
white, with black outer wing feathers and a pale yellowish wash
to the face in summer. The blue form retains the white head and
lower belly but is otherwise dark slate gray or brownish gray. In
both morphs its bill is thick at the base, is pink, and has a black
patch where the mandibles meet. Legs of both types are pink.
Snow Geese feed mostly on the ground, consuming shoots, roots,
grains, and insects. The similar Ross's Goose is smaller with a
shorter bill. A white morph adult is illustrated.

Canada Goose,
Branta canadensis
Family Anatidae
(Geese, Ducks, Mergansers)
Size: 27–32", depending on race
Season: Year-round
Habitat: Marshes, grasslands,
public parks, golf courses

The Canada Goose is the state's most common goose and is found
in suburban settings. It is vegetarian, foraging on land for grass,
seeds, and grain or in the water by upending like the dabbling
ducks. The Canada Goose has a heavy body with short, thick legs
and a long neck. Overall its coloring is barred gray-brown with a
white rear, short black tail, black neck, and white patch running
under the neck to behind the eyes. During the goose's powerful
flight, its white rump makes a semicircular patch between the tail
and back. Its voice is a loud honk. In flight Canada Geese form the
classic V formation. The adult is illustrated.

Tundra Swan,
Cygnus columbianus
Family Anatidae
(Geese, Ducks, Mergansers)
Size: 52"
Season: Winter
Habitat: Coastal estuaries,
shallow lakes, ponds

The Tundra Swan is Virginia's most widespread swan and also the smallest, wintering along coastal areas of North America and nesting in the tundra of the far north. It is white overall, sometimes stained with brown, except for a black bill and legs. The bill shows a variable-size patch of yellow just in front of the eyes, or this area may be completely black. Tundra Swans have long necks and bodies, with a forehead and crown that are quite rounded and an upper mandible that has a slightly concave profile. Juveniles are dusky gray with a pinkish bill. They forage for aquatic plants and animals, either on the ground or in the water. The adult is illustrated.

GEESE, DUCKS, MERGANSERS

Wood Duck, *Aix sponsa*
Family Anatidae (Geese, Ducks,
Mergansers)
Size: 18"
Season: Year-round
Habitat: Wooded ponds and swamps

The regal Wood Duck is among the dabbling ducks, or those that tip headfirst into shallow water to pluck aquatic plants and animals from the bottom. The male has a long tail and small bill, with a dark back, light buffy flanks, and sharp black-and-white head patterning. It also sports a bushy head crest that droops behind the nape. The female is gray-brown with spotting along the undersides and conspicuous white, teardrop-shaped eye patches. Both sexes swim with their heads angled downward as if in a nod, and they have sharp claws to cling to branches and snags. The illustration shows a breeding male (below), and a female (above).

Gadwall, *Anas strepera*
Family Anatidae (Geese, Ducks, Mergansers)
Size: 20.5"
Season: Year-round
Habitat: Shallow lakes, marshes

The Gadwall is a buoyant, plain-colored dabbling duck with a steep forehead and a somewhat angular head. The breeding male is grayish overall, with very fine variegation and barring. The rump and undertail coverts are black, the scapulars are light orange-brown, the tertials are gray, and the head is lighter below the eyes and darker above. Females and nonbreeding males are mottled brown with few distinguishing markings. In flight there is a distinctive white speculum that is most prominent in males. Gadwalls dabble or dive for a variety of aquatic plants and invertebrates and often gather in large flocks away from the shore. The breeding male (bottom) and female (top) are illustrated.

American Widgeon,
Anas americana
Family Anatidae
(Geese, Ducks, Mergansers)
Size: 19"
Season: Winter
Habitat: Shallow ponds, fields

The American Widgeon is also known as the Baldpate, in reference to its white crown. A wary and easily alarmed duck, it feeds from the water's surface, often gleaning prey stirred up by the efforts of diving ducks. The underside is a light cinnamon color with white undertail coverts, and the back is light brown. The male has a white crown and forehead with a very slight crest when seen in profile. A glossy dark green patch extends from the eyes to the back of the neck. A white wing covert patch can usually be seen on the folded wing, but is more obvious in flight. The head of the female is unmarked and brownish. The breeding male (bottom) and female (top) are illustrated.

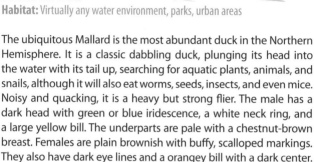

Mallard, *Anas platyrhynchos*
Family Anatidae (Geese, Ducks, Mergansers)
Size: 23"
Season: Year-round
Habitat: Virtually any water environment, parks, urban areas

The ubiquitous Mallard is the most abundant duck in the Northern Hemisphere. It is a classic dabbling duck, plunging its head into the water with its tail up, searching for aquatic plants, animals, and snails, although it will also eat worms, seeds, insects, and even mice. Noisy and quacking, it is a heavy but strong flier. The male has a dark head with green or blue iridescence, a white neck ring, and a large yellow bill. The underparts are pale with a chestnut-brown breast. Females are plain brownish with buffy, scalloped markings. They also have dark eye lines and a orangey bill with a dark center. The speculum is blue on both sexes, and the tail coverts often curl upward. Mallards form huge floating flocks called rafts. To achieve flight a Mallard lifts straight into the air without running. The breeding male (bottom) and a female (top) are illustrated.

Blue-winged Teal, *Anas discors*
Family Anatidae (Geese, Ducks, Mergansers)
Size: 16"
Season: Winter along the coast, spring and fall migrant inland
Habitat: Freshwater marshes and mud flats, wet agricultural areas

The Blue-winged Teal is a small duck that skims the water surface for aquatic plants and invertebrates, often forming large flocks. The male is mottled brown below with a prominent white patch near the hip area, dark above, and gray on the head, with a white vertical crescent at the base of the bill. The female is brownish with scalloped flanks and a plain head with dark eye lines and pale at the lores. Both sexes have light-blue wing patches visible in flight. The Blue-winged Teal is also known as the White-faced Teal. The breeding male (bottom) and female (top) are illustrated.

Northern Shoveler,
Anas clypeata
Family Anatidae (Geese, Ducks, Mergansers)
Size: 19"
Season: Winter
Habitat: Shallow marshes, lakes, and bays

Also known as the Spoonbill Duck, the Northern Shoveler skims the surface of the water with neck extended to scoop up aquatic animals and plants with its long, spatula-like bill. It will also suck up the ooze from mud and strain it through bristles at the edge of its bill to retain worms, leeches, and snails. This medium-size duck seems top heavy due to its large bill. Plumage in the male is white beneath with a large, chestnut-color side patch and a dark green head and gray bill. The female is pale brownish overall with an orangey bill. The breeding male (bottom) and female (top) are illustrated.

Northern Pintail,
Anas acuta
Family Anatidae (Geese, Ducks, Mergansers)
Size: 21"
Season: Winter
Habitat: Marshes, shallow lakes

Among the most abundant ducks in North America, the Northern Pintail is an elegant, slender dabbling duck with a long neck, small head, and narrow wings. In breeding plumage, the male has long pointed central tail feathers. It is gray along its back and sides, with a brown head and a white breast. A white stripe extends from the breast along the back of the neck. The female is mottled brown and tan overall, with a light brown head. To feed, the Northern Pintail bobs its head into the water to capture aquatic invertebrates and plants from the muddy bottom. It rises directly out of the water to take flight. The breeding male (bottom) and female (top) are illustrated.

Green-winged Teal, *Anas crecca*
Family Anatidae (Geese, Ducks, Mergansers)
Size: 14"
Season: Winter
Habitat: Marshes, ponds

The Green-winged Teal is a cute, very small, active duck with a small, thin bill. The breeding male is silvery gray with a dotted, tawny breast patch, a pale-yellow hip patch, and a distinct, vertical white bar on its side. The head is rusty brown with an iridescent green patch around and behind the eyes. Females and nonbreeding males are mottled brown with dark eye lines and white bellies. Green-winged Teals dabble in the shallows for plant material and small invertebrates. They are quick and agile in flight and sport a bright-green speculum. They form very large winter flocks. The breeding male (bottom) and female (top) are illustrated.

Redhead,
Aythya americana
Family Anatidae (Geese, Ducks, Mergansers)
Size: 19"
Season: Winter
Habitat: Shallow lakes, marshes, coastal bays

The Redhead is a heavy-bodied diving duck with a steep forehead and large, rounded head. The breeding male is pale gray with a dark rear end and breast. The head is light rusty brown, the eyes are yellow, and the bill is bluish with a black tip. The female is brownish gray overall, with pale areas at the base of the bill and throat. The upper side of the wing has white flight feathers and dark gray coverts. These birds "run" across the water to become airborne. They forage by diving for aquatic plants and invertebrates and may form huge, floating "rafts" during the winter. Redheads are similar in pattern to the larger Canvasbacks. The breeding male (bottom) and female (top) are illustrated.

Canvasback,
Aythya valisineria
Family Anatidae (Geese, Ducks, Mergansers)
Size: 21"
Season: Winter
Habitat: Grassy wetlands, lakes

The Canvasback is a stocky, thick-necked diving duck with a long, shallow forehead that slopes into the angle of the bill. The middle section of the breeding male, including back, wings, and belly, is entirely white. The tail and breast are black, and the head is a rusty brown that is darker on the crown and front of the face. The eyes are deep red. Females are very pale overall, with a light, canvas-colored back and a tan head and neck. The Canvasback runs across the water to take flight, where upon one can easily see the distinctive pattern of the light middle and darker ends. It usually feeds by diving for aquatic plants. The breeding male is illustrated.

Ring-necked Duck,
Aytha collaris
Family Anatidae (Geese, Ducks, Mergansers)
Size: 17"
Season: Winter
Habitat: Coastal marshes

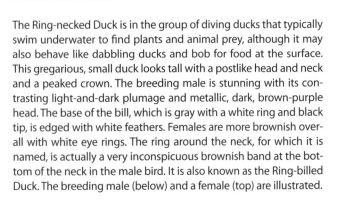

The Ring-necked Duck is in the group of diving ducks that typically swim underwater to find plants and animal prey, although it may also behave like dabbling ducks and bob for food at the surface. This gregarious, small duck looks tall with a postlike head and neck and a peaked crown. The breeding male is stunning with its contrasting light-and-dark plumage and metallic, dark, brown-purple head. The base of the bill, which is gray with a white ring and black tip, is edged with white feathers. Females are more brownish overall with white eye rings. The ring around the neck, for which it is named, is actually a very inconspicuous brownish band at the bottom of the neck in the male bird. It is also known as the Ring-billed Duck. The breeding male (below) and a female (top) are illustrated.

Lesser Scaup, *Aythya affinis*
Family Anatidae (Geese,
Ducks, Mergansers)
Size: 17"
Season: Winter
Habitat: Marshes, shallow lakes,
coastal bays

The Lesser Scaup is a small, short-bodied duck with a tall head profile and a relatively thin bill. The breeding male is distinctly two toned, with white sides; a pale, variegated gray back; and a black rear end and front. The head has a dark metallic violet or greenish cast in good light, and the bill has a small black dot at the nail. The nonbreeding male is paler, with brown on its sides. Females are gray-brown with a dark brown head and a white patch at the base of the bill. This diving duck forages for aquatic plants and insects. It is very similar to the Greater Scaup, but it is smaller and has a more peaked head. The breeding male (bottom) and female (top) are illustrated.

GEESE, DUCKS, MERGANSERS

Surf Scoter, *Melanitta perspicillata*
Family Anatidae (Geese, Ducks,
Mergansers)
Size: 20"
Season: Winter
Habitat: Coastal waters

The Surf Scoter is a stocky, large-headed coastal diving duck with short, pointed wings and a thick-based, colorful bill. The male is black overall, with white patches at the back of the neck and on the forehead. The eyes are light, and the bill is orange, with white on the sides with a round black spot. The female is brown-ish overall with a black cap, grayish bill, and faint white patches along the base of the bill and cheeks and sometimes on the nape. Surf Scoters dive for shellfish and crustaceans, propelled by their short wings. Because of their markings, they are sometimes called skunk-headed ducks. The breeding male (bottom) and female (top) are illustrated.

Long-tailed Duck,
Clangula hyemalis
Family Anatidae (Geese, Ducks, Mergansers)
Size: 16"(female), 21" (male)
Season: Winter
Habitat: Offshore coastal waters

Also known as the Oldsquaw, the Long-tailed Duck is a small sea duck with distinctive, long, thin central tail feathers (in males) that summers in the far north and Alaska. The winter male is boldly patterned white and black with silvery gray scapulars and flanks and a broad black breast band. The head is white with a gray face, darker cheek patches, and white eye rings, and two-toned black and pink bill. The female is dark brown above and on the breast, with a white face and black crown. Transitional states to summer plumage include an increasing amount of dark feathering. Long-tailed Ducks dive deep into the water (up to 200 feet), propelled by wings and feet, in search of marine invertebrates and plants. They voice a collection of noisey clucks or a loud, far-reaching yodel. The winter male (bottom) and female (top) are illustrated.

Bufflehead, *Bucephala albeola*
Family Anatidae (Geese, Ducks, Mergansers)
Size: 14"
Season: Winter
Habitat: Inland lakes or sheltered coastal bays

The Bufflehead is a diminutive diving duck; indeed it is the smallest duck in North America. Also known as the Bumblebee Duck, it forms small flocks that forage in the open water for aquatic plants and invertebrates. The puffy, rounded head seems large for the body and compared with the small, gray-blue bill. The breeding male is striking with a large white patch on the back half of its head, contrasting with the black front of its head and back. Its underside is white. The female is paler overall, with airfoil-shaped white patches behind the eyes on a dark, gray-brown head. Flight is low to the water, with rapid wing beats. The breeding male (bottom) and a female (top) are illustrated.

Common Goldeneye,
Bucephala clangula
Family Anatidae (Geese, Ducks, Mergansers)
Size: 18.5"
Season: Winter
Habitat: Lakes, rivers

The Common Goldeneye is a compact, large-headed diving duck with a tall, rounded head and a stubby bill. The breeding male is plumed in stark black and white; it has a white body with thin black streaks above and a black head and rear end. It has bright yellow eyes and a circular white patch between the eyes and the bill. The female is gray overall, with a brown head and a yellow-tipped bill. This duck is sometimes called the "Whistler" because of the whistling sound made by its wings in flight. It forms small flocks in the winter. The breeding male (bottom) and female (top) are illustrated.

Hooded Merganser,
Lophodytes cucullatus
Family Anatidae (Geese, Ducks, Mergansers)
Size: 18"
Season: Year-round
Habitat: Lakes, ponds, coastal waters

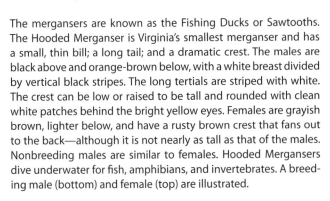

The mergansers are known as the Fishing Ducks or Sawtooths. The Hooded Merganser is Virginia's smallest merganser and has a small, thin bill; a long tail; and a dramatic crest. The males are black above and orange-brown below, with a white breast divided by vertical black stripes. The long tertials are striped with white. The crest can be low or raised to be tall and rounded with clean white patches behind the bright yellow eyes. Females are grayish brown, lighter below, and have a rusty brown crest that fans out to the back—although it is not nearly as tall as that of the males. Nonbreeding males are similar to females. Hooded Mergansers dive underwater for fish, amphibians, and invertebrates. A breeding male (bottom) and female (top) are illustrated.

Northern Bobwhite,
Colinus virginianus
Family Odontophoridae (Quail)
Size: 10"
Season: Year-round
Habitat: Brushy fields, open woodlands

The Bobwhite, like other quail, is a secretive, ground-dwelling bird that usually takes flight only if alarmed. It travels in coveys of ten or more while scavenging for seeds, berries, and insects. It is plump with a very short gray tail and a short, thick, curved bill. Its plumage is heavily streaked rufous, gray, and black, with a plain, rufous breast below a mottled black upper neck. It has a white superciliary stripe and throat. The female is paler with a greater extent of rufous coloring and buffy eye lines and throat. Call sounds somewhat like the bird's name: *bob-white*. The adult male is illustrated.

Ruffed Grouse,
Bonasa umbellus
Family Phasianidae (Turkeys, Grouse)
Size: 17"
Season: Year-round
Habitat: Mixed woodlands
of western mountains

The Ruffed Grouse is a cryptically colored ground bird with a thick body, rounded wings, longish tail, and small head that is often peaked in a triangular crest. Its plumage is mottled gray and brown above and on the head, with black-and-white spotting. The underside is white and heavily barred with black. Males have a black ruff about the neck that is held erect during display behaviors. Both sexes have a dark, subterminal tail band (often incomplete in females). Ruffed Grouse feed on the ground or in trees for seeds, berries, and buds. Their most distinctive sound is a repeated, low, muffled *whoompf,* increasing in tempo, that the male bird produces by pumping its wings together. The adult male is illustrated.

Wild Turkey,
Meleagris gallopavo
Family Phasianidae
(Turkeys, Grouse)
Size: 36–48"; male larger than female
Season: Year-round
Habitat: Open hardwood forests

The Wild Turkey is a very large (though slimmer than the domestic variety), dark ground-dwelling bird. The head and neck appear small for the body size and are covered with bluish, warty, crinkled bare skin that droops under the chin with a red wattle. The legs are thick and stout. The heavily barred plumage is quite iridescent in strong light. Often foraging in flocks, Wild Turkeys roam the ground for seeds, grubs, and insects and then roost at night in trees. Males emit the familiar *gobble*, while females are less vocal, with a soft *clucking* sound. In display the male hunches up with its tail up and spread like a giant fan. The adult male is illustrated.

Red-Throated Loon,
Gavia stellata
Family Gaviidae (Loons)
Size: 25"
Season: Winter
Habitat: Coastal bays, estuaries

The Red-throated Loon is Virginia's smallest loon and has a thin, pointed bill that it habitually holds at an upward tilted angle. The breeding adult is dark with white mottling above and white below. The head is pale gray with a rust throat patch and black-and-white striping down the nape. The bill is black. Nonbreeding adults lack the throat patch, their head is dark above the eyes and white across the face and foreneck, and their bill is pale gray. Red-throated Loons dive deep underwater in search of fish, propelled by their strong webbed feet. In flight Red-throated Loons hold their heads outstretched below the line of the body, and on land they are quite clumsy. The breeding (bottom) and nonbreeding (top) adult are illustrated.

Common Loon, *Gavia immer*
Family Gaviidae (Loons)
Size: 30"
Season: Winter
Habitat: Coastal waters

Riding low in the water outside the surf zone, the Common Loon, propelled by its strong webbed feet, periodically dives for fish. Designed for life in the water, this heavy bird has legs set far back on its body, which makes walking on land a clumsy affair and take-off into the air labored. This bird is usually seen in its drab, gray and white plumage, which is unlike the flashy, black-and-white spotted plumage it sports during the summer in northern lakes. Its call is a haunting yodel, but it is not commonly heard while in Virginia for the winter months. The Common Loon can be distinguished from other loons by the horizontal posture of its large bill (not held upward). It's fairly common in winter, scattered singly or in pairs along the coast. The nonbreeding (bottom) and breeding (top) adults are illustrated.

Horned Grebe, *Podiceps auritus*
Family Podicipedidae (Grebes)
Size: 14"
Season: Winter
Habitat: Coastal bays, inland marshes, lakes

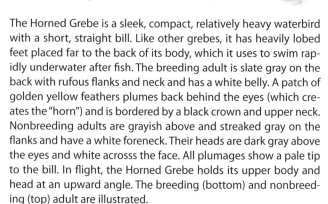

The Horned Grebe is a sleek, compact, relatively heavy waterbird with a short, straight bill. Like other grebes, it has heavily lobed feet placed far to the back of its body, which it uses to swim rapidly underwater after fish. The breeding adult is slate gray on the back with rufous flanks and neck and has a white belly. A patch of golden yellow feathers plumes back behind the eyes (which creates the "horn") and is bordered by a black crown and upper neck. Nonbreeding adults are grayish above and streaked gray on the flanks and have a white foreneck. Their heads are dark gray above the eyes and white acrosss the face. All plumages show a pale tip to the bill. In flight, the Horned Grebe holds its upper body and head at an upward angle. The breeding (bottom) and nonbreeding (top) adult are illustrated.

Pied-billed Grebe,
Podilymbus podiceps
Family Podicipedidae (Grebes)
Size: 13"
Season: Year-round
Habitat: Freshwater ponds
and lakes

The Pied-billed Grebe is a secretive, small grebe that lurks in sheltered waters, diving for small fish, leeches, snails, and crawfish. When alarmed or to avoid predatory snakes and hawks, it has the habit of sinking so that only the head is above water until danger has passed. It is brownish overall, slightly darker above, with a tiny tail and short wings. The breeding adult has a conspicuous dark ring around the middle of the bill, missing in winter plumage. It nests on a floating mat of vegetation. The breeding adult is illustrated.

Northern Gannet,
Morus bassanus
Family Sulidae (Gannets)
Size: 36"
Season: Winter
Habitat: Open ocean close to shore

The name *Gannet* comes from *gander* and alludes to the goose-like shape of this seabird. Often forming very large groups, the Northern Gannet alternates rapid wing beats with soaring flight. To feed, it forms its body into a sleek arrow shape and dramatically plunges headfirst into the ocean, completely submerging itself to catch fish. Its body is sleek and white with black flight feathers. The upper part of the head is pale yellow; the bill is thick, pointed, and bluish. The eyes seem small and are enveloped in a thin black ring and lores. The juvenile is dark and spotted with white. The adult is illustrated.

Double-crested Cormorant,

Phalacrocorax auritus
Family Phalacrocoracidae (Cormorants)
Size: 32"
Season: Year-round
Habitat: Open fresh water or salt water

Named for the two long white plumes that emerge from behind its eyes during breeding season, the Double-crested Cormorant is an expert swimmer that dives underwater to chase down fish. Because its plumage lacks the normal oils to repel water, it will stand with wings outstretched to dry itself. It is all black with a pale, glossy cast on the back and wings. The eyes are bright green, the bill thin and hooked, and the throat patch and lores yellow. The breeding adult is illustrated.

Great Cormorant,

Phalacrocorax carbo
Family Phalacrocoracidae (Cormorants)
Size: 36"
Season: Winter
Habitat: Coastal bays, estuaries, rocky shorelines

The Great Cormorant is Virginia's largest cormorant. It has a worldwide distribution but occurs in North America only along the North Atlantic coastline. It is a heavy bird with a thick bill and relatively large head and short, rounded tail. The nonbreeding plumage is all black with a bluish sheen, with paler scapular and back feathers bordered in black. The eyes are green, and there is a yellow gular patch behind the bill that is bordered by white feathers extending across the lower face and throat. Breeding adults have white facial plumes and a white patch at the flanks (especially noticeable in flight). Great Cormorants dive for fish, gripping them with their sharply hooked bills, and perch in small groups, often outstretching their wings to dry them. They fly with a distinct kink in their necks. The nonbreeding adult is illustrated.

Brown Pelican,
Pelecanus occidentalis
Family Pelecanidae
(Pelicans)
Size: 50"
Season: Year-round
Habitat: Coastal waters

The majestic Brown Pelican enlivens the coastal waters with its spectacular feeding process of plunge-diving headfirst for fish from some height. In flight it often cruises in formation inches from incoming swells, gaining lift and rarely needing to flap its wings. Its plumage is a bleached gray-brown overall with a white head and neck and a massive bill. In breeding, the head is pale yellow with a brown-red nape patch and a black strip down the back of the neck. Quite gregarious, the Brown Pelican may nest in mangrove trees or in slight depressions in the sand or rocks. The breeding adult is illustrated.

American Bittern,
Botaurus lentiginosus
Family Ardeidae (Herons, Egrets)
Size: 27"
Season: Year-round
Habitat: Marshy areas
with dense vegetation

The American Bittern is a fairly large, secretive heron with a small head; a long, straight bill; and a thick body. It has a habit of standing still with its neck and bill pointed straight up to imitate the surrounding reeds. Its plumage is very cryptic; above, it is variegated brown and tan, and below it is pale brown or whitish with thick, rust-colored streaking that extends up the neck. The bill is yellow-green and dark on the upper mandible. A dark patch extends from the lower bill to the upper neck. The legs are yellow-green and thick. American Bitterns skulk slowly through reeds and grasses to catch frogs, insects, and invertebrates. The adult is illustrated.

Least Bittern,
Ixobrychus exilis
Family Ardeidae (Herons, Egrets)
Size: 13"
Season: Summer
Habitat: Fresh or brackish marshes

The Least Bittern is Virginia's smallest heron. Secretive, this bird is more often heard than seen. It creeps and clambers through densely vegetated marshes searching for frogs, invertebrates, and other aquatic creatures, emitting a soft *cooing* or *kaw* when disturbed. It is rarely seen in flight. Its back is dark blue-gray; its midwing and body a buffy brown with white streaking. The crown is dark gray, and the bill is yellow and pointed. Legs and feet are yellow with long, thin toes for grasping clumps of vegetation. The female is paler along the back and crown. When alarmed it will stand motionless with its head straight up, imitating a stalk of reeds. The adult male is illustrated.

Great Blue Heron,
Ardea herodias
Family Ardeidae (Herons, Egrets)
Size: 46"
Season: Year-round
Habitat: Most aquatic areas, lakes, creeks, marshes

The Great Blue Heron is the largest heron in North America. Walking slowly through shallow water or fields, it stalks fish, crabs, and small vertebrates with the help of its massive bill. The Great Blue Heron has long legs and a long neck. It is blue gray overall, with a white face and heavy, yellow-orange bill. The crown is black and supports plumes of medium length. The front of the neck is white with distinct black chevrons fading into breast plumes. In flight the neck is tucked back and wing beats are regular and labored. The adult is illustrated.

Great Egret,
Ardea alba
Family Ardeidae (Herons, Egrets)
Size: 38"
Season: Year-round along
the coast, summer inland
Habitat: Fresh- or saltwater marshes

One of North America's most widespread herons, the Great Egret, is all white with a long, thin, yellow bill and long black legs. It develops long, lacy plumes across its back during breeding season. Stalking slowly, it pursues fish, frogs, and other aquatic animals. The breeding adult is illustrated.

Snowy Egret,
Egretta thula
Family Ardeidae (Herons, Egrets)
Size: 24"
Season: Summer
Habitat: Open water, marshes

The Snowy Egret is all white with lacy plumes across the back in breeding season. The bill is slim and black, and the legs are black with bright yellow feet. The juvenile has greenish legs with a yellow stripe along the front. It forages for fish and frogs along the shore by moving quickly, shuffling to stir up prey, and stabbing it. Sometimes it may run to pursue its prey. One can remember the name of this bird by thinking that it wears yellow "boots" because it is cold or "snowy." The breeding adult is illustrated.

Tricolored Heron,
Egretta tricolor
Family Ardeidae
(Herons, Egrets)
Size: 26"
Season: Year-round
Habitat: Salt marshes

The Tricolored Heron is a thin, bluish gray heron with a white belly and brownish neck stripe and lower back. In nonbreeding plumage it has yellow lores and an orangey bill, but in breeding season this area of the lores and bill are blue and the bill has a dark tip. It also develops plumes behind the ears and across the lower back. To feed, it will actively pursue prey or stand motionless, waiting to stab a fish or frog with its thin, spearlike bill. The breeding adult is ilustrated.

Cattle Egret,
Bubulcus ibis
Family Ardeidae
(Herons, Egrets)
Size: 20"
Season: Summer
Habitat: Upland fields,
often near cattle in grazing land

The Cattle Egret is a widespread species originally from Africa and now quite common in the Southeast. Unlike most herons, it is not normally found in aquatic environments. It forms groups around cattle, often perching atop them, and feeds on insects aroused by the movement of their hooves. It is stocky and all white with a comparatively short yellow bill and short black legs. In breeding plumage the legs and bill turn a bright orange, and a peachy, pale yellow forms on the crown, breast, and back. The nonbreeding adult is illustrated.

Green Heron,
Butorides virescens
Family Ardeidae
(Herons, Egrets)
Size: 18"
Season: Summer
Habitat: Ponds, creeks,
coastal wetlands (fresh water or salt water)

The Green Heron is a compact, crow-size heron that perches on low branches over the water, crouching forward to search for fish, snails, and insects. It is known to toss a bug into the water to help attract fish. The Green Heron is really not so green, but a dull grayish blue with a burgundy-chestnut–colored neck and black crown. The bill is dark, and the legs are bright yellow-orange. Fairly secretive and solitary, when disturbed it will erect its crest feathers, stand erect, and twitch its tail. The adult is illustrated.

Black-crowned Night-Heron,
Nycticorax nycticorax
Family Ardeidae (Herons, Egrets)
Size: 25"
Season: Year-round along the coast, summer inland
Habitat: Marshes, swamps with wooded banks

The nocturnal Black-crowned Night-Heron is a stocky, thick-necked heron with a comparatively large head and sharp, heavy, thick bill. It has pale gray wings, white underparts, and a black crown, back, and bill. The eyes are piercing red, and the legs are yellow. It develops long, white plumes on the rear of the head that are somewhat longer in breeding season. During the day it roosts in groups, but at night it forages alone, waiting motionless for prey such as fish or crabs. It may even raid the nests of other birds for their young. Its voice is composed of low-pitched barks and croaks. The adult is illustrated.

Yellow-crowned Night-Heron,
Nyctanassa violacea
Family Ardeidae (Herons, Egrets)
Size: 24"
Season: Summer
Habitat: Marshes, ponds, coastal shrubs

Shaped somewhat like the Black-crowned Night-Heron, the Yellow-crowned Night-Heron is blue-gray overall with a black face; white cheek patch; and slim, pale crown that is not really yellow but whitish or pale buff. In breeding plumage, it develops plumes from behind the crest. Its eyes are large and red, and its legs are yellow. The immature bird is drab brown-gray, mottled with light streaks. It is nocturnal, but will occasionally feed during the day for crustaceans and other aquatic animals, roosting in groups at night. The adult is illustrated.

White Ibis,
Eudocimus albus
Family Threskiornithidae (Ibises, Spoonbills)
Size: 25"
Season: Year-round
Habitat: Salt marshes, coastal swamps, fields

The White Ibis forages in groups, probing the mud and shallow water for small aquatic animals and invertebrates. It is all white except for the black tips of the primaries, which are rarely visible unless the wings are outstretched. The long, downward-curved bill is red with a darker tip and meets the face in unfeathered, reddish pink facial skin to the eyes. Legs are red. Juveniles are dark brown above, with a dark, streaky neck. Ibises fly with necks outstretched, unlike herons that fly with the neck folded back. The adult is illustrated.

Black Vulture,
Coragyps atratus
Family Cathartidae
(New World Vultures)
Size: 25"
Season: Year-round
Habitat: Open, dry country

Like the Turkey Vulture, the Black Vulture is adept at soaring. Its wing beats, however, are faster, and while soaring it holds its wings at a flat angle instead of a dihedral. It is stocky in physique; has a short, stubby tail; and has shorter wings than the Turkey Vulture. The primaries are pale on an otherwise black body, and the head is bald and gray. It eats carrion and garbage and is quite aggressive at feeding sites. The adult is illustrated.

Turkey Vulture,
Cathartes aura
Family Cathartidae
(New World Vultures)
Size: 27"
Season: Year-round
Habitat: Open, dry country

The Turkey Vulture is known for its effortless, skilled soaring. It will often soar for hours without flapping, rocking in the breeze on its long, 6-foot wings that form an upright V shape, or dihedral. It has a black body and inner wing with pale flight feathers and tail, which gives it a noticeable two-toned appearance from below. The tail is longish, and the feet extend to no more than halfway past the base of the tail. Its head is naked, red, and small, so the bird appears almost headless in flight. The bill is strongly hooked to aid in tearing apart its favored prey of carrion. Juveniles have a dark gray head. The Turkey Vulture often roosts in flocks and forms groups around food or at a roadkill site. The adult is illustrated.

Osprey,
Pandion haliaetus
Family Pandionidae (Osprey)
Size: 23"; female larger than male
Season: Summer
Habitat: Always near water, salt or fresh

Also known as the Fish Hawk, the Osprey exhibits a dramatic feeding method in which it plunges feet first into the water to snag fish. Sometimes it may completely submerge itself and then laboriously fly off with its heavy catch. It is dark brown above and white below and has distinct dark eye stripes contiguous with the nape. Females show a faint, mottled "necklace" across the breast, and juveniles have pale streaking on the back. Ospreys fly with an obvious crook at the wrist, appearing gull-like. Its wings are long and narrow, with a dark carpal patch. The adult is illustrated.

Northern Harrier,
Circus cyaneus
Family Accipitridae
(Kites, Hawks, Eagles)
Size: 18"; female larger than male
Season: Year-round along the coast, winter inland
Habitat: Open fields and wetlands

Also known as the Marsh Hawk, the Northern Harrier flies low to the ground, methodically surveying its hunting grounds for rodents and other small animals. When it spots prey, aided by its acute hearing, it will drop abruptly to the ground to attack. It is a thin raptor with long, flame-shaped wings that are broad in the middle and a long tail. The face has a distinct, owl-like facial disk, and there is a conspicuous white patch at the rump. Males are gray above with a white, streaked breast and black wing tips. Females are brown with a barred breast. Juveniles are similar in plumage to females but with a pale belly. The female (bottom) and male (top) are illustrated.

Bald Eagle,

Haliaeetus leucocephalus
Family Accipitridae
(Kites, Hawks, Eagles)
Size: 30–40"; female
larger than male
Season: Year-round
Habitat: Seashores, lakes,
rivers with tall perches or cliffs

The Bald Eagle is a large raptor that is widespread but fairly uncommon. It eats fish or scavenges dead animals and may congregate in large numbers where food is abundant. Its plumage is dark brown contrasting with a white head and tail. Juveniles show white splotching across the wings and breast. The yellow bill is large and powerful, and the talons are large and sharp. In flight it holds its wings fairly flat and straight, resembling a long plank. Bald Eagles make huge nests of sticks high in trees. The adult is illustrated.

Sharp-shinned Hawk,

Accipiter striatus
Family Accipitridae
(Kites, Hawks, Eagles)
Size: 10–14"; female larger than male
Season: Year-round
Habitat: Woodlands, bushy areas

The Sharp-shinned Hawk is Virginia's smallest accipiter, with a longish, squared tail and stubby, rounded wings. Its short wings allow for agile flight in tight, wooded quarters, where it quickly attacks small birds in flight. It is grayish above and light below, barred with pale rufous stripes. The eyes are set forward on the face to aid in the direct pursuit of prey. The juvenile is white below, streaked with brown. The Sharp-shinned Hawk may be confused with the larger Cooper's Hawk. The adult is illustrated.

Red-shouldered Hawk,

Buteo lineatus
Family Accipitridae
(Kites, Hawks, Eagles)
Size: 17"
Season: Year-round
Habitat: Wooded areas near water

The Red-shouldered Hawk is a solitary, small accipiterlike buteo with a long tail. It waits patiently on its perch before flying down to attack a variety of small animals. It has a banded black-and-white tail and spotted dark wings. The head and shoulder are rust colored, while the breast is heavily barred with rust, becoming paler toward the belly. Its legs are long and yellow, and its bill is hooked. In flight there is a pale arc just inside the wing tips, and it flaps with quick wing beats followed by short glides. The adult is illustrated.

Broad-winged Hawk,

Buteo platypterus
Family Accipitridae
(Kites, Hawks, Eagles)
Size: 15"
Season: Summer
Habitat: Woodlands, roadsides

The Broad-winged Hawk is Virginia's smallest buteo. It summers in eastern North America and migrates in huge flocks to Central and South America in the winter. It is dark brown above, white below, with a reddish brown breast that fades to spotting and barring across the belly and flanks. A rare dark morph is dark brown overall. Both morphs have wide black-and-white bars across the tail that is less developed in juveniles. In flight there is a dark border to the trailing edge of the otherwise light under-wing, and the wings are held flat while soaring. Broad-winged Hawks hunt for small mammals, reptiles, amphibians, or invertebrates, often near a water source. Their voice is a piercing, very high-pitched *pe-seeee*. The adult light morph is illustrated.

Red-tailed Hawk,
Buteo jamaicensis
Family Accipitridae
(Kites, Hawks, Eagles)
Size: 20"
Season: Year-round
Habitat: Open country, prairies

This widespread species is the most common buteo in the United States. It has broad, rounded wings and a stout, hooked bill. Its plumage is highly variable depending on geographic location. In general the underparts are light with darker streaking that forms a dark band across the belly, the upperparts are dark brown, and the tail is rufous. Light spotting occurs along the scapulars. In flight there is a noticeable dark patch along the inner leading edge of the underwing. Red-tailed Hawks glide down from perches, such as telephone poles and posts in open country, to catch rodents, and they may hover to spot prey. They are usually seen alone or in pairs. Voice is the familiar, *keeer!* The adult is illustrated.

FALCONS

American Kestrel,
Falco sparverius
Family Falconidae (Falcons)
Size: 10"
Season: Year-round
Habitat: Open country,
urban areas

North America's most common falcon, the American Kestrel is a tiny, robin-size falcon with long, pointed wings and tail. Fast in flight, it hovers above fields or dives from its perch on a branch or wire to capture small animals and insects. The upperparts are rufous and barred with black, the wings are blue-gray, and its breast is buffy or white streaked with black spots. The head is patterned with a gray crown and vertical patches of black down the face. The female has rufous wings and a barred tail. Also known as the Sparrow Hawk, it has a habit of flicking its tail up and down while perched. The adult male is illustrated.

Peregrine Falcon,

Falco peregrinus
Family Falconidae (Falcons)
Size: 17"; female larger
than male
Season: Winter
Habitat: Open country,
coastal cliffs, urban areas

The Peregrine Falcon is a powerful and agile raptor with long, sharply pointed wings. It is dark slate gray above and pale whitish below, with uniform barring below the breast. Plumage on the head forms a distinctive "helmet," with a white ear patch and chin contrasting with the blackish face and crown. Juveniles are mottled brown overall, with heavy streaking on the underside. Peregrine Falcons attack other birds in flight using spectacular high-speed aerial dives. Once threatened by DDT pollution that caused thinning of their eggshells, Peregrine Falcons have made a dramatic comeback. The adult is illustrated.

Black Rail,

Laterallus jamaicensis
Family Rallidae (Rails, Coots)
Size: 6"
Season: Summer
Habitat: Salt- or freshwater wetlands

The Black Rail is a rare, diminutive, secretive rail that is difficult to see as it skulks in dense, wetland vegetation. It is plump with a short tail and bill and has bright red eyes. The plumage is dark gray-brown above and slatey gray below, with white spotting across the back and flanks, and a rust patch across the upper shoulders. Both sexes and juveniles are similar. Black rails are active mostly at night, voicing a ragged *kik-a dow,* or a low cooing sound. They will often run rather than fly when disturbed. They forage among grasses for aquatic invertebrates, plants, and seeds. The adult is illustrated.

Clapper Rail,
Rallus longirostris
Family Rallidae (Rails, Coots)
Size: 14"
Season: Year-round
Habitat: Coastal salt water,
brackish marshes

Also known as the Marsh Hen, the Clapper Rail is very shy and difficult to see. It lurks through marshy vegetation and usually chooses to walk or swim rather than fly. It forages by probing through mud and grass for a variety of small prey, vocalizing harsh, clattering *kek-kek-kek* sounds in rapid succession. It is a relatively thin rail with a long, slightly decurved bill. The plumage is gray-brown above with a pale rust breast and barred flanks. The adult is illustrated.

Sora,
Porzana carolina
Family Rallidae (Rails, Coots)
Size: 9"
Season: Year-round
Habitat: Coastal marshes, meadows

The Sora is a small, short-tailed, chicken-shaped rail with long, thin toes. The plumage is mottled rusty brown above and gray-ish below, with white barring along the belly and sides. The head has a black patch between the eyes and bill, and the bill is yellow and conical. The tail is pointed and often cocked up and flicked. The juvenile is pale brown below, with less black on the face. Soras feed along shorelines or at the edges of meadows for snails, insects, and aquatic plants. Their voice is a soft, rising *ooo-eep,* and they are quite tame, being seen more often than other rails. The breeding adult is illustrated.

Virginia Rail, *Rallus limicola*
Family Rallidae (Rails, Coots)
Size: 9.5"
Season: Year-round
Habitat: Freshwater or brackish marshes

The Virginia Rail is a secretive, cryptic marsh bird about the size of a Sora but with a proportionately long, reddish, down-curved bill. The plumage is rusty brown overall, with darker streaking on the back and black-and-white barring about the flanks. The head has a dark crown and lores and a gray face. The legs are thick with long toes for support in the aquatic habitat. Virginia Rails are active mostly at dawn and dusk, skulking through vegetation, probing the mud for worms, aquatic invertebrates, and plants, and their voice is a quick, repetitive, two or three part *kik-kik*. They are similar in coloration to the much larger King Rails, which summer in eastern Virginia. The adult is illustrated.

American Coot, *Fulica americana*
Family Rallidae (Rails, Coots)
Size: 15"
Season: Year-round
Habitat: Wetlands, ponds, urban lawns, parks

The American Coot has a plump body and thick head and neck. It is a very common bird that becomes relatively tame in urban areas and parks and is most often seen swimming. It dives for fish to feed, but it will also dabble like a duck or pick food from the ground. The American Coot is dark gray overall, with a black head and a white bill that ends with a narrow dark ring. The white trailing edge of the wings can be seen in flight. The toes are flanked with lobes that enable the coot to walk on water plants and swim efficiently. Juveniles are similar in plumage but paler. Coots are often seen in very large flocks. The adult is illustrated.

Black-bellied Plover,
Pluvialis squatarola
Family Charadriidae (Plovers)
Size: 11"
Season: Winter
Habitat: Open areas, coastal or inland

The Black-bellied Plover is a relatively large plover with long, pointed wings and a whistling flight call. Like other plovers, it feeds by scooting quickly along the ground and stopping suddenly to peck at small prey in the mud or sand and then scooting along again. The winter plumage is gray above and paler below with a white belly. The bill is short, black, and thick. In flight there is a distinctive black patch on the axillary feathers. The breeding plumage develops a sharply contrasting black belly, face, and front of the neck. The breeding (bottom) and nonbreeding (top) are illustrated.

Piping Plover,
Charadrius melodus
Family Charadriidae (Plovers)
Size: 7"
Season: Summer
Habitat: Open sand
or mudflats, coastal beaches

The Piping Plover is rare and threatened due to disturbance to its open, sandy habitat. It is often heard before seen because of its cryptic coloration. It is a small plover with a short, thick bill. The plumage is pale sandy gray above and white below with a gray breast band. The legs are orange. In breeding plumage the breast band is black, there is a black patch above the forehead, and the bill turns orange with a black tip. Juveniles are similar to winter adults. In flight, the white tail coverts and wingbars are conspicuous. Piping Plovers scoot and stop across the sand, pecking for small invertebrates, and voice a sharp, high-pitched *pip-pip-pip or pee-low*. The breeding (bottom) and nonbreeding (top) adult are illustrated.

Killdeer,
Charadrius vociferus
Family Charadriidae (Plovers)
Size: 10"
Season: Year-round
Habitat: Inland fields,
farmlands, lakeshores, meadows

The Killdeer gets its name from the piercing *kill-dee* call that is often heard before this well-camouflaged plover is seen. Well adapted to human-altered environments, it is quite widespread and gregarious. It has long, pointed wings; a long tail; and a conspicuous double-banded breast. Its upperparts are dark brown, its belly is white, and its head is patterned with a white supercilium and forehead. The tail is rusty orange with a black tip. In flight there is a noticeable white stripe across the flight feathers. The killdeer is known for the classic "broken wing" display that it uses to distract predators from its nest and young. The adult is illustrated.

American Oystercatcher,
Haematopus palliatus
Family Haematopodidae
(Oystercatchers)
Size: 18"
Season: Year-round
Habitat: Coastal beaches, tide pools

The American Oystercatcher is a chunky, short-tailed, short-winged shorebird with a dark brown back, white belly, and black head. It has a heavy, knifelike, bright red bill; yellow eyes; and stocky, salmon-colored legs. In flight there is a distinct white bar across the secondary feathers. The American Oystercatcher follows the tidal pattern, foraging at low tide and roosting at high tide in groups with other shorebirds and gulls. It uses its bill to pry away shellfish—including oysters—from rocks or to probe for worms. The bill is also used to jam open bivalves and devour the flesh. Its voice is a loud, piping call. The adult is illustrated.

Black-necked Stilt,

Himantopus mexicanus
Family Recurvirostridae
(Avocets and Stilts)
Size: 14"
Season: Summer
Habitat: Shallow wetlands, marshes, lagoons

The Black-necked Stilt literally looks like a tiny body on stilts. It has extremely long, delicate, red legs and a thin, straight, needlelike black bill. The wings and mantle are black, and the underparts and tail are white. The head is dark above, with white patches above the eyes. The female has a slightly lighter, brownish back. In flight the long legs dangle behind the bird. To forage the Black-necked Stilt strides along to pick small prey from the water or vegetation, and it may voice a strident, barking *kek!* in alarm. Stilts are also known to perform the broken-wing or broken-leg act to distract predators. The adult male is illustrated.

Spotted Sandpiper,

Actitus macularius
Family Scolopacidae
(Sandpipers, Phalaropes)
Size: 7.5"
Season: Summer
Habitat: Streamsides, edges of lakes and ponds

The solitary Spotted Sandpiper is known for its exaggerated, constant bobbing motion. It has a compact body, long tail, and short neck and legs. Plumage is brown above and light below, with a white shoulder patch. There are white eye rings and superciliary stripes above the dark eye lines. In breeding plumage, the bird develops heavy spotting from the chin to lower flanks and barring on the back. The bill is orange with a dark tip. The Spotted Sandpiper has short wings, and in flight the thin white stripe on the upper wing can be seen. To forage, it teeters about, picking small water prey and insects from the shoreline. The breeding adult is illustrated.

Greater Yellowlegs,
Tringa melanoleuca
Family Scolopacidae
(Sandpipers, Phalaropes)
Size: 14"
Season: Winter along the coast;
spring and fall migrant inland
Habitat: Salt- or freshwater marshes

The Greater Yellowlegs is sometimes called the "tell-tale" bird, as the sentinel of a flock raises alarm when danger is near, flying off and circling to return. It has long, bright yellow legs; a long neck; a dark, slightly upturned bill; and white eye rings. The upperparts are dark gray and mottled, while its underparts are white with barring on the flanks. In breeding plumage the barring is noticeably darker and more extensive. To feed, the Greater Yellowlegs strides forward actively to pick up small aquatic prey or to chase fish. The Lesser Yellowlegs is similar but smaller. The nonbreeding adult is illustrated.

Willet, *Tringa semipalmatus*
Family Scolopacidae
(Sandpipers, Phalaropes)
Size: 15"
Season: Year-round
Habitat: Salt- or freshwater wetlands

The Willet is a heavy shorebird with a stout bill and conspicuous black-and-white wing markings in flight. It has overall mocha-brown plumage above and pale below, with extensive mottling in the breeding season. The Willet has white lores and eye rings, and its plain gray legs are thick and sturdy. It is found singly or in scattered flocks and picks or probes for crabs, crustaceans, and worms in the mud and sand. Its call is a loud *wil-let,* often uttered in flight. The nonbreeding adult is illustrated.

Marbled Godwit, *Limosa fedoa*
Family Scolopacidae
(Sandpipers, Phalaropes)
Size: 18"
Season: Winter along the coast;
spring and fall migrant inland
Habitat: Coastal beaches,
mudflats, marshes

As its name suggests, the Marbled Godwit is marbled, or barred, with dark across its buffy body, although the undersides lack marbling in winter plumage. The long, pinkish bill has a slight upcurved portion at the tip, where it becomes dark in color. The legs are dark, and the underwing is a rich cinnamon color. The bird also has a light superciliary stripe above dark eye lines. Marbled Godwits move about with slow, steady progress and probe in shallow water to find polychaete worms and crustaceans. Its call is a loud *god-wit!* The nonbreeding adult is illustrated.

Ruddy Turnstone, *Arenaria interpres*
Family Scolopacidae
(Sandpipers, Phalaropes)
Size: 9.5"
Season: Winter along the coast;
spring and fall migrant inland
Habitat: Rocky intertidal areas,
beaches, mudflats

The gregarious and frenetic Ruddy Turnstone is a chunky, short-legged shorebird with a short, wedge-shaped bill. The breeding adult has ruddy and black upperparts, a white belly, and a complex pattern of black and white on the head. The nonbreeding bird is pale brown and black above, with drab head markings. The stubby legs are orange. In flight the bird is white below and strongly patterned light and dark above. Turnstones bustle about constantly to pick, pry, or probe for almost any food item. Indeed it will "turn stones" to search for prey. The breeding (bottom) and nonbreeding (top) adult are illustrated.

Red Knot, *Calidris canutus*
Family Scolopacidae
(Sandpipers, Phalaropes)
Size: 10.5"
Season: Winter
Habitat: Coastal beaches, mudflats

The Red Knot is a compact, short-legged shorebird with a slightly down-curved bill. In nonbreeding plumage it is mottled gray-brown above and pale below with light streaking. In breeding plumage it has a rufous body with a grayish back and wings. The bill is dark, about the length of the head. In flight the long, pointed wings, which are gray underneath, can be seen. The Red Knot forages by probing and picking in the mud or sand for a variety of small prey. It often forms tight flocks while roosting and feeding. The breeding (bottom) and nonbreeding (top) adult are illustrated.

Sanderling, *Calidris alba*
Family Scolopacidae
(Sandpipers, Phalaropes)
Size: 8"
Season: Winter
Habitat: Coastal beaches, mudflats

The Sanderling is a common shorebird that runs back and forth following the incoming and outgoing surf, grabbing invertebrates exposed by the waves. It is a small, active, squat sandpiper with a short bill and legs. In nonbreeding plumage it is very pale above and white below, which contrasts with its black legs and bill. There is a distinct black shoulder and leading edge on the wing. Females in breeding plumage are speckled brown above, while males develop rufous on the back, head, and neck. A white wing stripe on the upper wing can be seen in flight. Sanderlings may form large foraging flocks and even larger flocks while roosting. The nonbreeding adult is illustrated.

Western Sandpiper, *Calidris mauri*

Family Scolopacidae
(Sandpipers, Phalaropes)
Size: 6.5"
Season: Winter
Habitat: Salt- and freshwater
wetlands, mudflats, coastal beaches

The Western Sandpiper is one of the "peeps," or very small sandpipers. It has a relatively long black bill that droops slightly and black legs. In winter it is pale gray-brown above and white below. In breeding plumage there is rufous on the scapulars and face and much darker streaking on the breast and back. A thin white stripe on the upper wing is visible in flight, along with a white rump with a dark central stripe. Western Sandpipers feed in shallow water or at the tide line, probing or picking invertebrates and insects. They often form rather large flocks. The nonbreeding (top) and breeding (bottom) adult are illustrated.

Dunlin, *Calidris alpina*

Family Scolopacidae
(Sandpipers, Phalaropes)
Size: 8.5"
Season: Winter along the coast; spring
and fall migrant inland
Habitat: Coastal beaches, mudflats

The name Dunlin comes from the word *dun,* which means a "dull, gray-brown color" and describes the winter plumage of this bird. The Dunlin is a rather small sandpiper with a long bill that droops down at the tip. In breeding plumage there is a black belly patch and rufous tones on the back. A white wing stripe on the upper wing and a white rump separated by a central dark line can be seen in flight. These birds form huge flocks, swirling and circling in unison. To feed they walk steadily through shallow waters, probing and picking crustaceans and other invertebrates. The breeding (bottom) and nonbreeding (top) adult are illustrated.

Wilson's Snipe, *Gallinago delicata*
Family Scolopacidae
(Sandpipers, Phalaropes)
Size: 10.5"
Season: Winter
Habitat: Salt- or freshwater marshes

Also known as the Common Snipe, the Wilson's Snipe is a cryptically marked, short-necked shorebird with a long, straight bill. The head is striped, and the back is flanked with white stripes bordering the scapulars. The underside is white with extensive black barring. The legs are short and pale greenish yellow. Plumage is similar in all seasons. While feeding, the Common Snipe probes rhythmically and deeply into the muddy substrate to extract worms, insect larvae, and crustaceans. Its voice is a loud *skipe!* when alarmed and a *whit, whit, whit, whit.* Secretive and solitary it will abruptly lift off in flight when alarmed. Its flight is erratic and zigzagging and includes "winnowing," a display where air across the tail feathers whistles during a steep descent. The adult is illustrated.

American Woodcock,
Scolopax minor
Family Scolopacidae
(Sandpipers, Phalaropes)
Size: 11"
Season: Year-round
Habitat: Upland woods, fields

The American Woodcock is a reclusive shorebird with a plump body, large head, long bill, stubby tail, and short legs. Its plumage is mottled gray above, with distinct, paler gray stripes down the sides of the back, and is plain buff to pale orange underneath. The head has two large black eyes set high up on the face and a dark crown with transverse buff stripes. Woodcocks are mostly active at night or dusk, probing soft soils for earthworms and insects. They voice a blunt nasal sound and produce a whistling noise in flight from air passing through their thin outer primary feathers. The adult is illustrated.

Bonaparte's Gull,
Chroicocephalus philadelphia
Family Laridae (Gulls, Terns)
Size: 13"
Season: Winter
Habitat: Coastal in winter;
inland during migration

The Bonaparte's Gull is a small gull named after the American ornithologist who was related to Napoleon. It is agile and ternlike in flight, skimming low over the water to snatch fish. It has a thin, sharp black bill and red legs. Plumage in breeding season includes a black head that contrasts with its white body and light gray back and wings. The primaries form a white triangle against the dark trailing edge in flight. The nonbreeding adult has a mostly white head with black eyes and a small dark spot around the ears. A solitary gull, it does not form large flocks, and its nest is made of sticks in evergreen trees. The breeding (bottom) and nonbreeding (top) adult are illustrated.

Laughing Gull,
Leucophaeus atricilla
Family Laridae (Gulls, Terns)
Size: 16"
Season: Year-round
Habitat: Coastal beaches and marshes,
urban environments, pastures

The Laughing Gull is so named because of its loud, often incessant laughing squawk. Social and uninhibited, it is a relatively thin, medium-size gull with long, pointed wings. The breeding adult has a black head with white eye arcs and a dark red bill. Upperparts are dark gray, underparts are white, and wing tips are black with small white dots at the ends. The nonbreeding adult has a white head with faint dark smudging behind the eyes. Laughing Gulls eat crabs, fish, and worms and will scavenge from humans for food or even steal from other birds. The breeding (bottom) and nonbreeding (top) adult are illustrated.

Ring-billed Gull,

Larus delewarensis
Family Laridae (Gulls, Terns)
Size: 18"
Season: Winter
Habitat: Lakes, ponds, parking lots

The Ring-billed Gull is common and quite tame. It is a relatively small gull with a rounded white head and a yellow bill with a dark subterminal ring. It has a pale gray back with black primaries tipped with white and has white underparts. The eyes are pale yellow, and the legs are yellow. The nonbreeding adult has faint streaking on the nape and around the eyes. Ring-billed Gulls feed from the water or on the ground, taking a wide variety of food, and may scavenge in urban areas and dumps. The nonbreeding adult is illustrated.

Herring Gull,

Larus argentatus
Family Laridae (Gulls, Terns)
Size: 25"
Season: Year-round
Habitat: Beaches, harbors, fields

The widespread Herring Gull occurs across the North American continent. It is a large, relatively thin, white-headed gull with a pale gray back and white underparts. The bill is thick and yellow with a reddish spot at the tip of the lower mandible. The primaries are black with white-spotted tips. The nonbreeding adult has brown streaking across the nape and neck. The legs are pink, and the eyes are pale yellow to ivory. The Herring Gull is an opportunistic feeder, eating fish, worms, crumbs, and trash. It is known to drop shellfish from the air to crack open the shells. The breeding (bottom) and nonbreeding (top) adult are illustrated.

GULLS, TERNS

Great Black-backed Gull,
Larus marinus
Family Laridae (Gulls, Terns)
Size: 29"
Season: Year-round
Habitat: Coastal beaches,
rocky shores, estuaries

The Great Black-backed Gull, the largest gull worldwide, has a large head and bill. The plumage is white with a dark, slate-gray back and wings marked with white-edged tertials and secondaries, and white tips of the outer primaries. The bill is yellow with a red spot on the lower mandible, and the legs are pink. Winter adults have minimal gray streaking on the top part of the head, and juveniles show extensive mottling and spotting on the back and breast. The Great Black-backed Gull feeds and scavenges on almost anything edible—including fish, mammals, birds, eggs, and invertebrates—and will dominate other species in mixed flocks. It will sometimes drop items from the air to crack or kill them. The breeding adult is illustrated.

Least Tern, *Sternula antillarum*
Family Laridae (Gulls, Terns)
Size: 9"
Season: Summer
Habitat: Sandy coastal shores

The Least Tern is the smallest North American tern and the only tern with a yellow bill and legs. It has a black cap and white forehead patch and is pale gray above and white below. The tail is forked, and the bill is tipped with black. Nonbreeding adults have a dark bill and more white on the front of the cap. In flight the wings are relatively narrow, and there is a black bar on the outer primaries. Least Terns often hover over the water before plunge-diving to catch small fish. They also pick worms and insects from the ground. This sensitive bird was once threatened by development of its coastal sandy breeding grounds. The breeding adult is illustrated.

Forster's Tern,
Sterna forsteri
Family Laridae (Gulls, Terns)
Size: 14"
Season: Year-round
Habitat: Coastal areas,
lakes, marshes

The Forster's Tern is a medium-size tern with no crest and a relatively long, pointed orange bill with a black tip. Breeding plumage is very pale gray above and white below, with a forked white tail and very light primaries. The head has a black cap, and the short legs are red. Nonbreeding adults have darker primaries, a black ear patch in place of the cap, and an all-black bill. Forster's Terns display swallowlike flight, with narrow pointed wings, and they plunge-dive for fish. They voice short, harsh one-syllable calls. The nonbreeding (top) and breeding (bottom) adult are illustrated.

Royal Tern,
Thalasseus maxima
Family Laridae (Gulls, Terns)
Size: 20"
Season: Year-round
Habitat: Coastal beaches,
salt marshes

The Royal Tern is a large but sleek tern with pointed, thin wings; a black, crested cap; and a red-orange, pointed bill. It is pale gray above and white below, with black legs. The nonbreeding adult has limited dark on the head, often reduced to a dark patch just behind the eyes. The dark outer primaries are visible in flight. The Royal Tern flies over the water surface, often hovering and then plunging down to catch fish. It breeds on sandbars in the company of thousands of other birds. The breeding (bottom) and nonbreeding (top) adult are illustrated.

Sandwich Tern,
Thalasseus sandvicensis
Family Laridae (Gulls, Terns)
Size: 15"
Season: Summer
Habitat: Coastal bays, esturaries,
offshore waters, islands

The Sandwich Tern is a streamlined, slender seabird that is similar in shape to the Royal Tern but quite a bit smaller. It has a long, thin black bill with a pointed yellow tip; forked wings; short black legs; and a ragged black crest. The plumage is pale, pearly gray above and white below with darker tips to the primaries (more visible in flight). The nonbreeding adults show white on the front half of the crown. Sandwich Terns plunge-dive into the ocean for fish, squid, or shrimp and may often be seen associating with Royal Terns, especially on breeding grounds. The breeding (bottom) and non-breeding (top) adult are illustrated

Black Skimmer, *Rynchops niger*
Family Laridae (Gulls, Terns)
Size: 18"
Season: Year-round
Habitat: Coastal bays, estuaries, rivers
and lakes just inland

The Black Skimmer has a most unique bill, in that the lower mandible is substantially longer than the upper mandible. The red bill is also thick at the base and knife-thin toward the end. This aids in the bird's foraging practice of flying just above the water's surface, wings held above the body, with the mouth open and the lower mandible cutting a furrow through the water. When it encounters something solid, the Black Skimmer's mouth slams shut and, hopefully, the bird catches a fish. Plumage is black on the back, wings, and crown and white below. The legs are tiny and red. Nonbreeding adults have a white nape, contiguous with the white of the body. The breeding adult is illustrated.

Rock Pigeon,
Columba livia
Family Columbidae (Pigeons, Doves)
Size: 12"
Season: Year-round
Habitat: Urban areas, farmland

The Rock Pigeon (also known as the Rock Dove) is the common pigeon seen in almost every urban area across the continent. Introduced from Europe, where they inhabit rocky cliffs, Rock Pigeons here have adapted to city life, and domestication has supplied a huge variety of plumage colors and patterns. The original wild version is a stocky gray bird with a darker head and neck and green to purple iridescence along the sides of the neck. The eyes are bright red, and the bill has a fleshy white cere on the base of the upper mandible. There are two dark bars across the back when the wing is folded, the rump is white, and the tail has a dark terminal band. Variants range from white to brown to black, with many pattern combinations. The adult is illustrated.

Mourning Dove,
Zenaida macroura
Family Columbidae (Pigeons, Doves)
Size: 12"
Season: Year-round
Habitat: Open brushy areas, urban areas

The common Mourning Dove is a sleek, long-tailed dove with a thin neck, a small rounded head, and large black eyes. Underneath it is pale gray-brown and darker above, with some iridescence to the feathers on the neck. There are clear black spots on the tertials and some coverts, and there is a dark spot on the upper neck below the eyes. The pointed tail is edged with a white band. The Mourning Dove pecks on the ground for seeds and grains and walks with quick, short steps while bobbing its head. Flight is strong and direct, and the wings create a whistle as the bird takes off. Its voice is a mournful, owl-like cooing. It is usually solitary or found in small groups, but it may form large flocks where food is abundant. The adult is illustrated.

Yellow-billed Cuckoo,
Coccyzus americanus
Family Cuculidae (Cuckoos)
Size: 12"
Season: Summer
Habitat: Woodlands,
streamsides, swamps

Like the other cuckoos, the Yellow-billed Cuckoo is secretive and shy, hiding in vegetation, where it picks insects, caterpillars, and fruit from trees. It is brown above, with rufous flight feathers, and crisp white below. The bill is yellow with black along the top ridge. The tail is long and gradated with large white spots on the underside. The voice is a dry, repetitive *kak kak kak,* or a low, owl-like *kwoo, kwoo.* The adult is illustrated.

Barn Owl,
Tyto alba
Family Tytonidae (Barn Owls)
Size: 23"
Season: Year-round
Habitat: Barns, farmland,
open areas with mature trees

The Barn Owl is a large-headed pale owl with small dark eyes, a heart-shaped facial disk, and long feathered legs. The wings, back, tail, and crown are light rusty brown with light gray smudging and small white dots. The underside, face, and underwing linings are white, with spots of rust on the breast. Females are usually darker than males, with more color and spotting across the breast and sides. The facial disk is enclosed by a thin line of darker feathers. Barn Owls are nocturnal hunters for rodents, and their call is a haunting, raspy *screeee!* The adult male is illustrated.

Eastern Screech-Owl,
Megascops asio
Family Strigidae (Typical Owls)
Size: 8.5"
Season: Year-round
Habitat: Wooded areas or parks; places where cavity-bearing trees exist

The Eastern Screech-Owl is a small, big-headed, eared owl with a short tail and bright yellow eyes. The highly camouflaged plumage ranges from reddish to brown to gray, depending on the region, but the red form is most common in the East. It is darker above, streaked and barred below. The ear tufts may be drawn back to give a rounded head appearance, and the bill is grayish green tipped with white. White spots on the margins of the coverts and scapulars create two white bars on the folded wing. The Eastern Screech-Owl is a nocturnal bird, hunting during the night for small mammals, insects, or fish. Its voice is a descending, whistling call or a rapid staccato of one pitch. The red morph adult is illustrated.

Great Horned Owl,
Bubo virginianus
Family Strigidae (Typical Owls)
Size: 22"
Season: Year-round
Habitat: Forests, plains, urban areas

Found throughout North America, the Great Horned Owl is a large, strong owl with an obvious facial disk and sharp, long talons. Plumage is variable, but eastern forms are brown overall with heavy barring, a rust-colored face, and a white chin patch. The prominent ear tufts give the owl its name, and the eyes are large and yellow. The Great Horned Owl has exceptional hearing and sight. It feeds at night, perching on branches or posts, then swooping down on silent wings to catch birds, snakes, or mammals up to the size of a cat. Its voice is a low *hoo-hoo-hoo*. The adult is illustrated.

Barred Owl,
Strix varia
Family Strigidae (Typical Owls)
Size: 21"
Season: Year-round
Habitat: Wooded swamps, upland forests

The Barred Owl is a large, compact owl with a short tail and wings, rounded head, and big dark eyes. It lacks the ear tufts seen on the Great Horned Owl and has comparatively small talons. Plumage is gray-brown overall with dark barring on the neck and breast, turning to streaking on the belly and flanks. It swoops from its perch to catch small rodents, frogs, or snakes. Its voice, often heard during the day, is a hooting, *who-cooks-for-you,* or kind of bark. It makes its nests in tree cavities vacated by other species. The adult is illustrated.

Common Nighthawk,
Chordeiles minor
Family Caprimulgidae (Nightjars, Nighthawks)
Size: 9"
Season: Summer
Habitat: Forests, marshes, plains, urban areas

The Common Nighthawk is primarily nocturnal, but may often be seen flying during the day and evening hours, catching insects on the wing with bounding flight. It is cryptically mottled gray, brown, and black, with strong barring on an otherwise pale underside. In the male a white breast band is evident. The tail is long and slightly notched, and the wings are long and pointed, extending past the tail in the perched bird. In flight there is a distinct white patch on both sides of the wings. During the day the Common Nighthawk is usually seen roosting on posts or branches with its eyes closed. Its voice is a short, nasal, buzzing sound. The adult male is illustrated.

Chuck-will's-widow,
Caprimulgus carolinensis
Family Caprimulgidae
(Nightjars, Nighthawks)
Size: 12"
Season: Summer
Habitat: Woodland areas with clearings

Chuck-will's-widow is a highly camouflaged, fairly large nightjar with a fat head, big dark eyes, and a tiny bill. The body is thick and broad around the midsection, giving it a hunched appearance. It is overall rusty or brown-gray, spotted and streaked with black. There are pale edges to the scapulars and a pale chin stripe above the dark breast. The tail is long and projects beyond the primaries. In flight its long, pointed wings and white on the outer tail feathers in the male can be seen. Chuck-will's-widow is nocturnal, feeding at night by springing from its perch or the ground for flying insects. During the day it roosts on the ground or in trees with its eyes closed. Its voice is somewhat like its name, *chuck-wil-wi-dow*. The adult is illustrated.

Chimney Swift,
Chaetura pelagica
Family Apodidae (Swifts)
Size: 5"
Season: Summer
Habitat: Woods, scrub, swamps, urban areas

The gregarious Chimney Swift is unrelated to the swallows but similar in shape. The body is like a fat torpedo with a very short tail and long, pointed, bowed wings that bend close to the body. It is dark brown overall and slightly paler underneath and at the chin. Constantly on the wing, it catches insects in flight with quick wing beats and fast glides. It never perches, but roosts at night on vertical cliffs, on trees, or in chimneys. Its voice is a quick chattering uttered in flight. The adult is illustrated.

Ruby-throated Hummingbird,

Archilochus colubris
Family Trochilidae (Hummingbirds)
Size: 3.5"
Season: Summer
Habitat: Areas with flowering plants, gardens, urban feeders

The Ruby-throated Hummingbird is a small, delicate bird able to hover on wings that beat at a blinding speed. The long, needle-like bill is used to probe deep into flowers so the bird can lap up the nectar. Its feet are tiny, and its body is white below and green above. Males have a dark green crown and iridescent red throat, or gorget. Females lack the colored gorget and have a light green crown and white-tipped tail feathers. Their behavior is typical of hummingbirds, hovering and buzzing from flower to flower, emitting chits and squeaks. Most of these birds migrate across the Gulf of Mexico to South America in the winter. The adult male (bottom) and female (top) are illustrated.

Belted Kingfisher,

Megaceryle alcyon
Family Alcedinidae (Kingfishers)
Size: 13"
Season: Year-round
Habitat: Creeks, lakes, sheltered coastlines

The widespread but solitary Belted Kingfisher is a stocky, large-headed bird with a powerful, long bill and shaggy crest. It is grayish blue-green above and white below, with a thick blue band across the breast and white dotting on the back. At the lores is a white spot. The female has an extra breast band of rufous and rufous along the flanks. Belted Kingfishers feed by springing from a perch along the water's edge or hovering above the water and then plunging head-first to snatch fish, frogs, or tadpoles. Its flight is uneven, and its voice is a raspy, rattling sound. The adult female is illustrated.

Red-headed Woodpecker,
Melanerpes erythrocephalus
Family Picidae (Woodpeckers)
Size: 9"
Season: Year-round
Habitat: Woodlands, areas with standing dead trees, suburbs

The Red-headed Woodpecker has a striking bright red head and a powerful, tapered bill. It is black above, with a large patch of white across the lower back and secondaries, and white below. The juvenile has a pale brown head and incomplete white back patch. In all woodpeckers the tail is very stiff, with sharp tips to aid in support while clinging to a tree trunk. To feed, the Red-headed Woodpecker pecks at bark for insects, but may also fly out to snatch its prey in midair. It will also take nuts and store them in tree cavities for winter. This species has been losing nesting cavities since the introduction of the European Starling. The adult is illustrated.

Red-bellied Woodpecker,
Melanerpes carolinus
Family Picidae (Woodpeckers)
Size: 9"
Season: Year-round
Habitat: Woodlands, wooded swamps, parks, urban areas

The Red-bellied Woodpecker is a fairly common, large-billed woodpecker with extensively barred back and wings. The underparts are pale buff with a barely discernable hint of rose on the belly that gives the bird its name. The crown and nape are reddish orange. Females lack the red crown, and juveniles have an entirely gray head. Like all woodpeckers, the Red-bellied Woodpecker has two toes that point forward and two toes that point backward to allow a secure grip on tree trunks as it pecks away bark to find insects. It also feeds on nuts and oranges. Its flight is undulating wing beats and glides. The adult is illustrated.

Downy Woodpecker, *Picoides pubescens*
Family Picidae (Woodpeckers)
Size: 6.5"
Season: Year-round
Habitat: Woodlands, parks,
urban areas, streamsides

The Downy Woodpecker is a tiny woodpecker with a small bill and relatively large head. It is white underneath with no barring, has black wings barred with white, and has a patch of white on the back. The head is boldly patterned white and black, and the male sports a red nape patch. The base of the bill joins the head with fluffy nasal tufts. Juveniles may show some red on the forehead and crown. The Downy Woodpecker forages for berries and insects in the bark and smaller twigs of trees. The very similar Hairy Woodpecker is larger with a longer bill and more aggressive foraging behavior, sticking to larger branches and not clinging to twigs. The adult male is illustrated.

Pileated Woodpecker,
Dryocopus pileatus
Family Picidae (Woodpeckers)
Size: 16.5"
Season: Year-round
Habitat: Old-growth forests, urban areas with large trees

The Pileated Woodpecker is North America's largest woodpecker, except for the probably extinct huge Ivory-billed Woodpecker. It is a very large, powerful, long-necked, and crested bird. The body is all black with a white base to the primaries, which are mostly covered in the folded wing. The head is boldly patterned black and white, with a bright red crest that is limited on the female. The male has a red malar patch instead of the black of the female. The contrasting white wing lining can be seen in flight. To forage, Pileated Woodpeckers chip away chunks of bark to uncover ants and beetles, but will feed on berries during winter months. Its voice is a high-pitched, uneven, resounding *wok-wok-wok*. The adult male is illustrated.

Northern Flicker,
Colaptes auratus
Family Picidae (Woodpeckers)
Size: 12.5"
Season: Year-round
Habitat: Suburbs, parks

The common Northern Flicker is a large, long-tailed woodpecker often seen foraging on the ground for ants and other small insects. It is barred brown and black across the back and buff with black spotting below. The head is brown with a gray nape and crown and a small red patch behind. On the upper breast is a prominent half-circle of black, and the male has a black patch at the malar region. Its flight is undulating and shows a golden yellow wing lining and white rump. The flicker's voice is a loud, sharp *keee,* and it will sometimes drum its bill repeatedly at objects like a jackhammer. The adult male is illustrated.

PASSERINES

Eastern Wood-Pewee,
Contopus virens
Family Tyrannidae (Tyrant Flycatchers)
Size: 6.25"
Season: Summer
Habitat: Woodland edges, canyons, creeksides

The Eastern Wood-Pewee is a large-headed, thick-necked fly-catcher with drab plumage overall. It is brownish gray or olive-gray, with pale whitish or dusky underparts and gray sides that meet at the breast. Very slight eye rings surround the dark eyes, and the bill is thin and pointed and has a pale lower mandible. There are thin wing bars along the coverts and edges of the ter-tials. The Eastern Wood-Pewee is nearly identical to the Western Wood-Pewee, but their ranges do not normally overlap. Eastern Wood-Pewees flycatch for insects; they start from a high perch and then return to the same spot. Its voice is composed of shrill, high-pitched *pee-wee* notes. The adult is illustrated.

Acadian Flycatcher,

Empidonax virescens
Family Tyrannidae (Tyrant Flycatchers)
Size: 6"
Season: Summer
Habitat: Wooded riparian areas

TYRANT FLYCATCHERS

The Acadian Flycatcher is a member of the sometimes-confusing Empidonax group that breeds throughout the southeastern United States. It has a relatively long, robust bill; long wings; and thin eye rings, and the hind crown often shows a slight peak. Its color is olive green above and whitish below, with variable amounts of pale yellow wash on the lower belly and a faint greenish breast band. The wings are dark with pale wing bars and edges to the tertials. Both sexes and juveniles are similar. Acadian Flycatchers flycatch for insects within the tree canopy, and may also eat berries. The song is a high-pitched, sharp *peet-see,* rising on the second syllable. The adult is illustrated.

Eastern Phoebe, *Sayornis phoebe*
Family Tyrannidae (Tyrant Flycatchers)
Size: 7"
Season: Summer; year-round in southeastern Virginia
Habitat: Brushy streamsides

The Eastern Phoebe is a compact, large-headed flycatcher with a thin, pointed bill and a long tail that it habitually pumps up and down. The plumage is grayish across the back, wings, tail, and head, with darker areas on the face and crown. The underparts are white, sometimes washed with pale yellow on the belly, with a bit of gray extending onto the sides of the breast. The wing bars are quite dull, and there are no distinct eye rings. Sexes are similar, and juveniles show more yellow on the underparts. Eastern Phoebes flycatch for insects from branch tips or fence wires, and they sing a song that sounds somewhat like its name, *fee-bee,* or a series of chattering *sit* notes. The adult is illustrated.

Great Crested Flycatcher,
Myiarchus crinitus
Family Tyrannidae (Tyrant Flycatchers)
Size: 8.5"
Season: Summer
Habitat: Open woodlands and scrub, urban areas

The Great Crested Flycatcher is a large flycatcher with a proportionately large head and full crest. The upperparts and head are olive-brown, and the throat and breast are gray with a bright yellow belly. The primaries and tail show rufous color, while the margins to the tertials and coverts are white. Both sexes and juveniles are similar in plumage. The yellow wing linings and rufous tail are seen in flight. The Great Crested Flycatcher feeds by flying from perch to perch, catching insects in flight. It is often seen erecting its crown feathers and bobbing its head. Its voice is a high-pitched, whistling *wheeeerup!* The adult is illustrated.

Eastern Kingbird,
Tyrannus tyrannus
Family Tyrannidae (Tyrant Flycatchers)
Size: 8.5"
Season: Summer
Habitat: Open woodlands, agricultural and rural areas

The Eastern Kingbird is a medium-size, slender flycatcher. Upperparts are bluish black, and underparts are white with a pale gray breast. The dark head cap contrasts with the white lower half of the face. The tail is black with a white terminal band. The Eastern Kingbird flies with shallow wing beats on wings that are mostly dark and pointed. It perches on wires, treetops, or posts and takes flight to capture insects on the wing. Its voice is a distinctive series of very high-pitched, sputtering, zippy *psit* notes. The adult is illustrated.

Loggerhead Shrike,
Lanius ludovicianus
Family Laniidae (Shrikes)
Size: 9.5"
Season: Year-round
Habitat: Dry open country

The solitary Loggerhead Shrike is raptorlike in its feeding habits. It swoops down from its perch on a branch, wire, or post and captures large insects, small mammals, or birds, impaling them on thorny barbs before tearing them apart to feed. It is a compact, large-headed bird with a short, thick, slightly hooked bill. The upperparts are gray and the underparts are pale. The wings are black with white patches at the base of the primaries and upper coverts. The tail is black and edged with white. A black mask on the head extends from the base of the bill to the ear area. Juveniles show a finely barred breast. Flight is composed of quick wing beats and swooping glides. The adult is illustrated.

White-eyed Vireo,
Vireo griseus
Family Vireonidae (Vireos)
Size: 5"
Season: Summer
Habitat: Dense woodlands, thickets, shrubs

The White-eyed Vireo is a small, chunky vireo with a relatively large head and short bill. It is grayish olive green above and pale gray below, tinged with yellow on the flanks and undertail coverts. The head is grayish with conspicuous yellow "spectacles," or combined lores and eye ring area. The large eyes are white. On the wings are two white wing bars. Juveniles have darker eyes than that of adults. This bird gleans insects, spiders, and berries from the dense vegetation. The adult is illustrated.

Blue-headed Vireo,
Vireo solitarius
Family Vireonidae (Vireos)
Size: 5.5"
Season: Winter near the coast;
summer in the west
Habitat: Woodlands, urban areas
with trees

The Blue-headed Vireo was once grouped with the Plumbeous and Cassin's Vireo as one species, the Solitary Vireo. It is olive-gray above and white below, tinged with yellow on the sides and flanks. The head is blue-gray with white "spectacles" and a white chin. There are two white or pale yellow wing bars on the wing coverts. It gleans insects and berries in the upper tree canopies. Its voice consists of short, high-pitched phrases. The adult is illustrated.

Red-eyed Vireo, *Vireo olivaceus*
Family Vireonidae (Vireos)
Size: 6"
Season: Summer
Habitat: Areas of dense vegetation,
mature deciduous forests

The Red-eyed Vireo is a sluggish, slow-moving bird that haunts the upper tree canopy, picking out insects and berries. Its head appears rather flat, and its tail is short. It is light olive green above and white below, with a yellow wash across the breast, flanks, and undertail coverts. It has dark eye lines, white eyebrows, and a grayish crown. The eyes are red, and the bill is fairly large with a hooked tip. Its voice is a repetitive, incessant song in single phrases. The adult is illustrated.

Blue Jay, *Cyanocitta cristata*
Family Corvidae (Jays, Crows)
Size: 11"
Season: Year-round
Habitat: Woodlands, rural and urban areas

The solitary Blue Jay is a sturdy, crested jay. It is bright blue above and white below, with a thick, tapered black bill. There are white patches around the eyes to the chin, bordered by a thin black "necklace" that extends to the back of the nape. It has a conspicuous white wing bar and dark barring on the wings and tail. In flight the white outer edges of the tail are visible as the bird alternates shallow wing beats with glides. Omnivorous, the Blue Jay eats just about anything, especially acorns, nuts, fruits, insects, and small vertebrates. It is a raucous and noisy bird and quite bold. Sometimes it mimics the calls of birds of prey. The adult is illustrated.

American Crow,
Corvus brachyrhynchos
Family Corvidae (Jays, Crows)
Size: 17.5"
Season: Year-round
Habitat: Open woodlands, pastures, rural fields, dumps

The American Crow is a widespread corvid found across the continent voicing its familiar, loud, grating *caw, caw*. It is a large, stocky bird with a short, rounded tail; broad wings; and a thick, powerful bill. Plumage is overall glistening black in all stages. The American Crow will eat almost anything, often forming loose flocks with other crows. The adult is illustrated.

Fish Crow,
Corvus ossifragus
Family Corvidae (Jays, Crows)
Size: 15"
Season: Year-round
Habitat: Coastal marshes, rivers, agricultural areas

The Fish Crow is virtually identical to the American Crow but smaller, glossier overall, and restricted to the southeastern United States. It has a softer, nasal *ah-hah* voice and prefers to forage on fish and crustaceans. The adult is illustrated.

Common Raven,
Corvus corax
Family Corvidae (Jays, Crows)
Size: 24"
Season: Year-round
Habitat: Mountains, canyons, and forests of western Virginia

The Common Raven is a stocky, gruff, large corvid with a long, massive bill that slopes directly into the forehead. The wings are narrow and long, and the tail is rounded or wedge shaped. The entire body is glossy black, sometimes bluish, and the neck is laced with pointed, shaggy feathers. Quite omnivorous, it feeds on carrion, refuse, insects, and roadkill and has a varied voice that includes deep croaking. Ravens may soar and engage in rather acrobatic flight. Crows are similar but are smaller with proportionately smaller bills. The adult is illustrated.

Horned Lark,
Eremophila alpestris
Family Alaudidae (Larks)
Size: 7"
Season: Year-round
Habitat: Open and barren country

The Horned Lark is a slim, elongated, ground-dwelling bird with long wings. The plumage is pale reddish gray above and whitish below, with variable amounts of rusty smudging or streaking on the breast and sides. The head is boldly patterned with a black crown, cheek patch, and breast bar, contrasting with a yellow throat and white face. In females the black markings are much paler. Particularly evident on males are feather tufts, or "horns," on the sides of the crown. Outer tail feathers are black. Horned Larks scurry on the ground, foraging for plant matter and insects, and sing with rapid, musical warbles and chips. The adult male is illustrated.

Purple Martin, *Progne subis*
Family Hirundinidae (Swallows)
Size: 8"
Season: Summer
Habitat: Marshes, open water, agricultural areas

The Purple Martin is the largest North American swallow. It has long, pointed wings; a streamlined body; and a forked tail. The bill is very short and broad at the base. The male is dark overall with a blackish blue sheen across the back and head, while the female is paler overall with sooty, mottled underparts. Flight consists of fast wing beats alternating with circular glides. Purple Martins commonly use human-made nest boxes or tree hollows to nest. The adult male is illustrated.

Tree Swallow, *Tachycineta bicolor*
Family Hirundinidae (Swallows)
Size: 5.75"
Season: Year-round near the coast; summer in western mountains
Habitat: Variety of habitats near water and perching sites

The Tree Swallow has a short, slightly notched tail; broad-based triangular wings; and a thick neck. It has a high-contrast plumage pattern with dark metallic green-blue upperparts and crisp white underparts. When the bird is perched, the primaries reach just past the tail tip. Juveniles show gray-brown below with a subtle, darker breast band. Tree Swallows take insects on the wing, but they will also eat berries and fruits. They often form huge lines of individuals perched on wires or branches. Their voice is a high-pitched chirping. The adult male is illustrated.

Northern Rough-winged Swallow,

Stelgidopteryx serripennis
Family Hirundinidae (Swallows)
Size: 5.5"
Season: Summer
Habitat: Sandy cliffs, steep streamsides, outcrops, bridges

The Northern Rough-winged Swallow flies in a smooth and even fashion, with full wing beats, feeding on insects caught on the wing. It is uniform brownish above and white below. The breast is lightly streaked with pale brown, and the tail is short and square. Juveniles show light rust-colored wing bars on the upper coverts. These fairly solitary swallows find nesting sites in holes in sandy cliffs. The adult is illustrated.

Barn Swallow, *Hirundo rustica*
Family Hirundinidae (Swallows)
Size: 6.5"
Season: Summer
Habitat: Open rural areas near bridges, old buildings, and caves

The widespread and common Barn Swallow has narrow, pointed wings and a long, deeply forked tail. It is pale below and dark blue above with a rusty orange forehead and throat. In males the underparts are pale orange, while in females they are pale cream below. Barn Swallows are graceful, fluid fliers, and they often forage in groups while catching insects in flight. Their voice is a loud, repetitive chirping or clicking. They build a cup-shaped nest of mud on almost any protected human-made structure. The adult male is illustrated.

Carolina Chickadee,

Poecile carolinensis
Family Paridae (Chickadees, Titmice)
Size: 4.75"
Season: Year-round
Habitat: Woodlands, rural gardens

The Carolina Chickadee is a small, compact, active bird with short, rounded wings. It is gray above and lighter gray or dusky below, with a contrasting black cap and throat patch. It is quite similar to the Black-capped Chickadee, which occurs in more mountainous habitats. Voice sounds like the name, *chick-a-dee, dee, dee,* or a soft *fee-bay.* The Carolina Chickadee is quite social and feeds on a variety of seeds, berries, and insects found in trees and shrubs. The adult is illustrated.

Tufted Titmouse,
Baeolophus bicolor
Family Paridae (Chickadees, Titmice)
Size: 6.5"
Season: Year-round
Habitat: Woodlands, urban areas

The tame and curious Tufted Titmouse is a small, chunky bird with short, broad wings and a conspicuous tuft on the crest. It is gray above and pale gray below, with a wash of orange along the sides and flanks. It has a small but sturdy black bill, large black eyes, and a black forehead. It often forms foraging groups with other species who flit through the vegetation picking out nuts, seeds, insects, and berries from the bark and twigs. At feeders, the Tufted Titmouse prefers sunflower seeds. Its voice is a repetitive *peeta peeta*. The adult is illustrated.

White-breasted Nuthatch,
Sitta carolinensis
Family Sittidae (Nuthatches)
Size: 5.75"
Season: Year-round
Habitat: Mixed oak and coniferous woodlands

The White-breasted Nuthatch has a large head and wide neck, short rounded wings, and a short tail. It is blue-gray above and pale gray below, with rusty smudging on the lower flanks and undertail coverts. The breast and face are white, and there is a black crown that merges with the mantle. The bill is long, thin, and upturned at the tip. To forage, the nuthatch creeps headfirst down tree trunks to pick out insects and seeds. It nests in tree cavities high off the ground. Voice is a nasal, repetitive *auk, auk, auk*. The adult male is illustrated.

NUTHATCHES

Brown-headed Nuthatch,
Sitta pusilla
Family Sittidae (Nuthatches)
Size: 4.5"
Season: Year-round
Habitat: Pine woodlands

The Brown-headed Nuthatch is a compact, short-necked, large-headed bird with a short stubby tail. It feeds by clinging to tree trunks and creeping its way down headfirst, picking out insects, larvae, or seeds from the bark. The legs are short, but the toes are long to help it grasp the bark. The bill is long, thin, sharp, and upturned at the tip. Plumage is gray above and lighter gray or buffy below. On the head are a brown cap, dark eye lines, and a small white spot on the back of the nape. The nuthatch has undulating flight and nests in cavities in tree trunks. The adult is illustrated.

Carolina Wren,
Thryothorus ludovicianus
Family Troglodytidae (Wrens)
Size: 5.5"
Season: Year-round
Habitat: Understory of wooded and brushy areas, swamps

The Carolina Wren is a vocal but cryptic bird, usually hidden among dense foliage close to the ground. It lurks in vegetation, picking out insects, seeds, or fruit and emitting a musical song or a harsh, quick call. The body is plump with a short rounded tail and a thin, slightly downcurved bill. It is dark rusty brown above, buffy below, and has a long white superciliary stripe that extends to the nape. Wings and tail are thinly barred with black. This bird habitually holds its tail in a cocked-up position. The adult is illustrated.

House Wren, *Troglodytes aedon*
Family Troglodytidae (Wrens)
Size: 4.75"
Season: Year-round in southeast Virginia;
summer elsewhere
Habitat: Shrubby areas, rural gardens

The House Wren is a loud, drab wren with short rounded wings and a thin, pointed, downcurved bill. Plumage is brown and barred above and pale gray-brown beneath, with barring on the lower belly, undertail coverts, and tail. The head is lighter on the throat, at the lores, and above the eyes. House Wrens feed in the brush for insects and sing rapid, melodic chirping songs, often while cocking their tails downward. The adult is illustrated.

Marsh Wren, *Cistothorus palustris*
Family Troglodytidae (Wrens)
Size: 5"
Season: Year-round
Habitat: Marshes, reeds, streambanks

The Marsh Wren is a small, cryptic, rufous-brown wren with a normally cocked-up tail. The tail and wings are barred with black, and the chin and breast are white. There is a well-defined white superciliary stripe below a uniform brown crown, and the mantle shows distinct black-and-white striping. The bill is long and slightly decurved. Marsh Wrens are vocal day and night with quick, repetitive cheeping. They are secretive but inquisitive and glean insects from the marsh vegetation and water surface. The adult is illustrated.

Blue-gray Gnatcatcher,

Polioptila caerulea
Family Polioptilidae (Gnatcatchers)
Size: 4.5"
Season: Summer
Habitat: Deciduous or pine woodlands, thickets

The Blue-gray Gnatcatcher is a tiny, energetic, long-tailed bird with a narrow, pointed bill and thin dark legs. It is blue-gray above and pale gray below with white edges to the terials creating a light patch on the middle of the folded wing. The tail is rounded and has black inner and white outer feathers. The eyes are surrounded by crisp, white eye rings. Males are brighter blue overall and have a darker surpraloral line. To forage, gnatcatchers flit through thickets and catch insects in the air. They will often twitch and fan their tails. Voice is a high-pitched buzzing or cheep sound, which sometimes sounds like the call of other birds. The adult male is illustrated.

Golden-crowned Kinglet,

Regulus satrapa
Family Regulidae (Kinglets)
Size: 4"
Season: Year-round in the high mountains; winter elsewhere
Habitat: Mixed woodlands, brushy areas

The Golden-crowned Kinglet is a tiny, plump songbird with a short tail and a short, pointed bill. It is greenish gray above and green, and pale gray below, with wings patterned in black, white, and green. The face has dark eye stripes and crown, and the center of the crown is golden yellow and sometimes raised. The legs are dark with orange toes. Kinglets are in constant motion, flitting and dangling among branches, sometimes hanging upside down or hovering at the edge of branches to feed. Voice includes very high-pitched *tzee* notes. The adult is illustrated.

Eastern Bluebird,
Sialia sialis
Family Turdidae (Thrushes)
Size: 7"
Season: Year-round
Habitat: Open woodland, pastures, fields

The Eastern Bluebird is a member of the thrush family that travels in small groups, feeding on a variey of insects, spiders, and berries and singing a series of musical *chur-lee* notes. It is a stocky, short-tailed, short-billed bird that often perches in an upright posture on wires and posts. The male is brilliant blue above and rusty orange below, with a white belly and undertail region. The orange extends to the nape, making a subtle collar. The female is paler overall with a white throat and eye rings. Juveniles are brownish gray with extensive white spotting and barred underparts. Human-made nest boxes have helped this species increase in numbers throughout its range. The adult male (bottom) and female (top) are illustrated.

Hermit Thrush, *Catharus guttatus*
Family Turdidae (Thrushes)
Size: 7"
Season: Summer in the western highlands, winter elsewhere
Habitat: Woodlands, brushy areas

The Hermit Thrush is a compact, short-tailed thrush that habitually cocks its tail. It forages on the ground near vegetative cover for insects, worms, and berries and voices its song of beautiful, flutelike notes. It is reddish to olive-brown above with a rufous tail. Underparts are white with dusky flanks and sides and black spotting on the throat and breast. The dark eyes are encircled by complete, white eye rings. In flight the pale wing lining contrasts with the dark flight feathers. The adult is illustrated.

Wood Thrush, *Hylocichla mustelina*
Family Turdidae (Thrushes)
Size: 7.75"
Season: Summer
Habitat: Dense, mixed woodlands;
suburban areas

The Wood Thrush is a solitary, fairly plump thrush with a short tail and relatively large bill. It is rich reddish orange on the head, fading to a duller brown across the back and tail. Below, it is white with extensive dark spotting from the throat down to the flanks. There are distinct white eye rings and a black-and-white streaked auricular patch. The legs are thin and pale pink. Sexes are similar. Wood Thrushes hop through the undergrowth and along the ground for insects, worms, or berries and voice a beautiful, fluting song preceded by short soft notes. The adult is illustrated.

American Robin,
Turdus migratorius
Family Turdidae (Thrushes)
Size: 10"
Season: Year-round
Habitat: Widespread in a variety of
habitats including woodlands, fields,
parks, lawns

Familiar and friendly, the American Robin is a large thrush with a long tail and legs. It commonly holds its head cocked and keeps its wing tips lowered beneath its tail. It is gray-brown above and rufous below, with a darker head and contrasting white eye crescents and loral patch. The chin is streaked black and white, and the bill is yellow mixed with darker edges. Females are typically paler overall, and juveniles show white spots above and dark spots below. Robins forage on the ground, picking out earthworms and insects, or in trees to find berries. Song is a series of high musical phrases like *cheery, cheeruup, cheerio*. The adult male is illustrated.

Gray Catbird, *Dumetella carolinensis*
Family Mimidae (Mockingbirds, Catbirds, Thrashers)
Size: 8.5"
Season: Year-round in eastern Virginia; summer elsewhere
Habitat: Understory of woodland edges, shrubs, rural gardens

The solitary Gray Catbird is long-necked and sleek with a sturdy, pointed bill. It is uniformly gray except for its rufous undertail coverts, black crown, and black rounded tail. It is quite secretive and spends most of its time hidden in thickets close to the ground, picking through the substrate for insects, berries, and seeds. Call includes a nasal, catlike *meew* from which its name is derived, although it also mimics the songs of other birds. To escape danger it will often choose to run away rather than fly. The adult is illustrated.

Northern Mockingbird,
Mimus polyglottos
Family Mimidae (Mockingbirds, Catbirds, Thrashers)
Size: 10.5"
Season: Year-round
Habitat: Open fields, grassy areas near vegetative cover, suburbs, parks

The Northern Mockingbird is constantly vocalizing. Its scientific name, *polyglottos,* means "many voices," alluding to its amazing mimicry of the songs of other birds. It is sleek and has a long tail and legs. Plumage is gray above, with darker wings and tail, and off-white to brownish gray below. It has two white wing bars; short, dark eye stripes, and pale eye rings. In flight conspicuous white patch on the inner primaries and coverts and white outer tail feathers can be seen. Like other mimids, the mockingbird forages on the ground for insects and berries, intermittently flicking its wings. The adult is illustrated.

Brown Thrasher,

Toxostoma rufum
Family Mimidae (Mockingbirds, Catbirds, Thrashers)
Size: 11"
Season: Year-round in eastern Virginia; summer in the west
Habitat: Woodlands, thickets, urban gardens, orchards

The Brown Thrasher is primarily a ground-dwelling bird that thrashes through leaves and dirt for insects and plant material. It has a long tail and legs with a medium-length, slightly decurved bill. Plumage is rufous-brown above, including the tail, and whitish below, heavily streaked with brown or black. There are two prominent pale wing bars and pale outermost corners to the tail. Its eyes are yellow to orange. Voice is a variety of musical phrases, often sung from a conspicuous perch. The adult is illustrated.

European Starling,

Sturnus vulgaris
Family Sturnidae (Starlings)
Size: 8.5"
Season: Year-round
Habitat: Almost anywhere, particularly rural fields, gardens, dumps, urban parks

Introduced from Europe, the European Starling has successfully infiltrated most habitats in North America and competes with native birds for nest cavities. It is a stocky, sturdy, and aggressive bird that is overall glossy black with a sheen of green or purple. The breeding adult has a yellow bill and greater iridescence, while the winter adult is colored a more flat black with a black bill and numerous white spots. The tail is short and square. Starlings form very large, compact flocks and fly directly on pointed, triangular wings. The diet is highly variable and includes insects, grains, and berries. Voice consists of loud, wheezy whistles and clucks and imitations of other birdsongs. The breeding adult is illustrated.

Cedar Waxwing,
Bombycilla cedrorum
Family Bombycillidae (Waxwings)
Size: 7"
Season: Year-round
Habitat: Woodlands, swamps, urban areas near berry trees

The Cedar Waxwing is a compact, crested songbird with pointed wings and a short tail. The sleek, smooth plumage is brownish gray overall with paler underparts, a yellowish wash on the belly, and white undertail coverts. The head pattern is striking, with a crisp black mask thinly bordered by white. The tail is tipped with bright yellow, and the tips of the secondary feathers are coated with a unique red waxy substance. Cedar Waxwings will form large flocks and devour berries from one tree and then move on to the next. They may also flycatch for small insects. Voice is an extremely high-pitched whistling *seee*. The adult is illustrated.

Golden-winged Warbler,
Vermivora chrysoptera
Family Parulidae (Wood-Warblers)
Size: 4.75"
Season: Summer in western Virginia; spring and fall migrant elsewhere
Habitat: Woodland edges, brushy fields

The Golden-winged Warbler has a long, thin, sharp bill that it uses to extract and pick insects and larvae. Plumage is gray above and pale gray or whitish below, and there are white outer corners to the tail. Yellow wing coverts create a broad yellow patch on the upper wings. Males have a striking black facial mask and throat with a yellow forecrown. Females are patterned similarly but with a gray mask and throat and a grayer yellow crown. These warblers build nests in thickets on the ground. The breeding male (bottom) and female (top) are illustrated.

Northern Parula,
Parula americana
Family Parulidae (Wood-Warblers)
Size: 4.5"
Season: Summer
Habitat: Treetops in woodlands

The Northern Parula is a tiny, stubby warbler with a short, sharp bill; short tail; and relatively large head. Upperparts are slatey blue with a greenish mantle. Below there is a white belly and undertail, a yellow chin and breast, and a rufous breast band. Above and below the eyes are white eye arcs, and the lower mandible is yellow. The wings show two bold, white wing bars. The female is bordered above the breast band with gray. Northern Parulas forage for insects and caterpillars in trees. The adult male is illustrated.

Chestnut-sided Warbler,
Dendroica pensylvanica
Family Parulidae (Wood-Warblers)
Size: 5"
Season: Summer in western highlands; spring and fall migrant elsewhere
Habitat: Early growth forest, shrubby fields, abandoned pasture

The Chestnut-sided Warbler is a distinctly colored warbler that breeds in upland Virginia and often perches with its tail slightly cocked. Adults in summer plumage are streaked black and pale yellow across the back and are white below, with a chestnut band along the sides. The head has a bright yellow crown and black eye lines and moustacial stripe. Females are less chestnut on the sides and less dark on the face. Winter adults are greenish yellow across the back and head, with no dark on the face. Chestnut-sided Warblers flit through the low understory, gleaning spiders and insects, and sing a series of high, soft notes ending with an accented *wee-choo!* The breeding (bottom) and nonbreeding (top) male are illustrated.

Magnolia Warbler, *Dendroica magnolia*

Family Parulidae (Wood-Warblers)
Size: 4.75"
Season: Summer in western highlands;
spring and fall migrant elsewhere
Habitat: Coniferous woodlands

The Magnolia Warbler is a relatively plump, boldly patterned warbler with a longish tail and short bill. The plumage is medium gray above and bright yellow below and on the rump, with white undertail coverts. The breeding male has a broad black stripe through the face and onto the mantle and thick black streaking on the breast and flanks. There is also a white patch at the wing coverts and behind the eyes. The nonbreeding male has an all gray upper head with less extensive black on the back and breast. Females are somewhat intermediate between breeding and nonbreeding males. Magnolia Warblers remain in the cover of vegetation, foraging for insects. Song is a melody of short, cheery *weet* or *weet-chee* phrases. The breeding (bottom) and nonbreeding (top) male are illustrated.

Black-throated Blue Warbler, *Dendroica caerulescens*

Family Parulidae (Wood-Warblers)
Size: 5"
Season: Summer
Habitat: Upland woodlands with dense undergrowth

The Black-throated Blue Warbler is a compact, thick-necked warbler with striking sexual dimorphism. The male is steely blue above and white below, with a black face, throat, sides, and flanks. The female is drab olive-gray above and pale olive-yellow below, with a dark auricular patch and a thin white supercilium and lower eye arcs. Noticeable in flight or while perched, the white wing patch at the base of the primaries is unique among warblers. Warblers forage primarily for insects in the lower canopy and sing a series of high-pitched, raspy *ze-ze-zhweee* notes, accented and higher at the end. The breeding male (bottom) and female (above) are illustrated.

Blackburnian Warbler,
Dendroica fusca
Family Parulidae (Wood-Warblers)
Size: 5"
Season: Summer in western Virginia; spring and fall migrant elsewhere
Habitat: Mature coniferous or mixed woodlands

The Blackburnian Warbler is a beautifully colored and boldly patterned warbler with a relatively large head and neck. The breeding male is black above with extensive white on the wing coverts and whitish streaks on the back. The underside progresses from bright yellow-orange on the head and throat, to yellow on the breast, to white toward the rear. The head has a black crown and facial pattern, and there is black streaking down the sides. The female has similar patterning but is duller overall with less orange and less white on the wing coverts. Blackburnian Warblers perch and forage high in the tree canopy, feeding on insects, and sing a series of extremely high-pitched *tsee* or *sit* notes. The breeding male (bottom) and female (top) are illustrated.

Yellow-throated Warbler,
Dendroica dominica
Family Parulidae (Wood-Warblers)
Size: 5.25"
Season: Summer
Habitat: Coniferous and mixed woodlands near water

The Yellow-throated Warbler is an elongated, long-billed warbler that forages high in the tree canopy, picking insects from the bark. The plumage is slate-gray above and white below and is heavily streaked with black. The chin and breast are a clean yellow. The warbler has a bold face pattern with a white supercilium and lower eye arcs bordered by black eye stripes and auricular areas. Behind the ears are distinctive white patches. The dark back contrasts with two white wing bars. The outer tail feathers show patches of white. The adult male is illustrated.

Pine Warbler, *Dendroica pinus*
Family Parulidae (Wood-Warblers)
Size: 5.5"
Season: Year-round
Habitat: Pine and mixed pine
woodlands

The Pine Warbler has a rounded shape, long wings, and a relatively thick bill. The plumage is olive green above and yellow streaked with olive below. The wings are gray and the belly and undertail coverts are white. The yellow of the chin extends under the auricular areas; a faint "spectacle" is formed by the light lores and eye rings, and there are two clearly marked white wing bars. Females are paler overall, and juveniles lack yellow on the chin and underparts. The outer tail feathers show white patches. The Pine Warbler creeps along pine branches picking insects from the bark. The adult male is illustrated.

Prairie Warbler,
Dendroica discolor
Family Parulidae (Wood-Warblers)
Size: 4.5"
Season: Summer
Habitat: Mangroves, early succession
forests, shrubs

The Prairie Warbler is a small, plump, long-tailed warbler with a rising, buzzy song, sometimes sung from a treetop perch. It is olive green above and bright yellow below, with black streaking along its sides topped by a distinct spot just behind the bottom of the chin. Dark half-circles swoop underneath the eyes, and sometimes rusty streaking is seen on the mantle. The female is slightly paler overall. The outer tail feathers are white. Prairie Warblers forage through low branches of the understory for insects and spiders. The adult male is illustrated.

WOOD-WARBLERS

Black-and-white Warbler,
Mniotilta varia
Family Parulidae (Wood-Warblers)
Size: 5.25"
Season: Summer
Habitat: Mixed woodlands

WOOD-WARBLERS

The Black-and-white Warbler is a unique warbler that behaves more like a nuthatch, creeping up and down tree trunks probing for insects in the bark with its long, downcurved bill. The breeding male, like its name suggests, is streaked black and white overall, with a black throat, auricular patches, and crown, topped with a thin white medial stripe. Females have paler streaking on the undersides, a white throat, gray auriculars, and buff flanks. Both sexes have black spotting on the undertail coverts. Voice is a series of high-pitched *see-see-see* notes or a quick *seeta-seeta-seeta*. The breeding male (bottom) and female (top) are illustrated.

American Redstart,
Setophaga ruticilla
Family Parulidae (Wood-Warblers)
Size: 5"
Season: Summer
Habitat: Open mixed woodlands in early succession

The constantly active, frenetic American Redstart often fans its tail and wings in display while perched. It has a long tail, and the plumages of males and females are markedly different. The male is jet black above, white below, with a fiery red patch at the side of the breast, and a paler, peachy red wing bar and sides of the tail. The female is gray-green above with a slatey gray head and white chin and breast. The colored areas are located in the same areas of the male but are yellow. Redstarts eat insects gleaned from branches and bark or flycatch for insects. The adult male (bottom) and female (top) are illustrated.

Prothonotary Warbler,
Protonotaria citrea
Family Parulidae (Wood-Warblers)
Size: 5.5"
Season: Summer
Habitat: Wooded swamps

Also known as the Golden Swamp Warbler, the Prothonotary Warbler is a fairly large warbler with a short tail, relatively large head, and long, sharp bill. The head and underparts are a rich yellow to yellow-orange, and the undertail coverts are white. The wings and tail are blue-gray, and the mantle is olive green. Females and juveniles are paler overall, with an olive cast to the head. Prothonotary Warblers forage through the understory for insects. The adult male is illustrated.

Worm-eating Warbler,
Helmitheros vermivorum
Family Parulidae (Wood-Warblers)
Size: 5.25"
Season: Summer
Habitat: Dense growth in woodlands, often near streams

The Worm-eating Warbler is a plain-looking, relatively large warbler with a short, stubby tail and a thick, long bill. The sexes are similar in plumage, which is olive-brown above and pale buff below, with no apparent wing bars or tail spots. The only obvious markings are on the head, which has two thin black crown stripes and thin black eye lines. The legs are pale pinkish or flesh colored. Worm-eating Warblers forage on or close to the ground for insects and caterpillars, not necessarily just worms, as the common name would imply. Their song is a rapid trill of dry, toneless, buzzy notes. The adult is illustrated.

Louisiana Waterthrush,

Parkesia motacilla
Family Parulidae (Wood-Warblers)
Size: 6"
Season: Summer
Habitat: Wooded areas near streamsides

The Louisiana Waterthrush is a large warbler (not a thrush) of aquatic environments with long legs, a long bill, and a relatively short tail. Both sexes have similar plumage, which is dark brown above and whitish below with brown streaking across the breast, sides, and flanks. The head is patterned with a dark crown, eye stripes, and auricular patches and with a broad white supercilium, malar region, and throat. The legs are long, thin, and pinkish. The Louisiana Waterthrush forages on streambanks for insects or aquatic invertebrates, habitually bobbing its tail. The adult is illustrated.

Common Yellowthroat,

Geothlypis trichas
Family Parulidae (Wood-Warblers)
Size: 5"
Season: Summer
Habitat: Low vegetation near water, swamps, fields

The Common Yellowthroat scampers through the undergrowth for insects and spiders in a somewhat wrenlike manner. It is a plump little warbler that often cocks up its tail. Plumage is olive-brown above, pale brown to whitish below, with bright yellow undertail coverts and breast/chin. The male has a black facial mask trailed by a fuzzy white area on the nape. Females lack the facial mask. The adult male (bottom) and female (top) are illustrated.

Hooded Warbler,
Wilsonia citrina
Family Parulidae (Wood-Warblers)
Size: 5"
Season: Summer
Habitat: Moist woodlands, swamps

The Hooded Warbler lurks in the woodland understory picking out insects while continually flicking its tail and singing its high, musical *weeta-weeta-weeta-toe*. Plumage is olive green above and bright yellow below. The male has a full black hood that encompasses the face and chin, while the female has a fainter partial mask with a yellow chin. White inner vanes to the outer tail feathers can be seen in the fanned tail. The adult male (bottom) and female (top) are illustrated.

Yellow-breasted Chat,
Icteria virens
Family Parulidae (Wood-Warblers)
Size: 7.5"
Season: Summer
Habitat: Dense vegetation, woodland edges

The largest wood-warbler, the Yellow-breasted Chat has a long rounded tail and a heavy, black, pointed bill with a strongly curved culmen. The plumage is uniformly greenish brown above; below, the belly and undertail coverts are white and the chin and breast are bright yellow. The head is dark with bold white patterning above the lores, at the malar area, and around the eyes, forming white "spectacles." Females are slightly duller in color. Yellow-breasted Chats forage in low brush for insects and berries and have quite variable vocalizations, including mimicking the songs of other birds. The male has a strange display behavior in which it hovers and dangles the legs. The adult is illustrated.

Eastern Towhee,
Pipilo erythrophthalmus
Family Emberizidae (Sparrows)
Size: 8"
Season: Year-round
Habitat: Thickets, suburban shrubs, gardens

SPARROWS

The Eastern Towhee is a large, long-tailed sparrow with a thick, short bill and sturdy legs. It forages on the ground in dense cover by kicking back both feet at once to uncover insects, seeds, and worms. The Eastern Towhee is black above, including the head and upper breast, and has rufous sides and a white belly. The base of the primaries is white, as are the corners of the tail. Eye color ranges from red to white, depending on the region. Females are like the males but are brown above. Song is a musical *drink-your-teee*. The Eastern Towhee was once conspecific with the Spotted Towhee as the Rufous-sided Towhee. The adult male is illustrated.

Chipping Sparrow, *Spizella passerina*
Family Emberizidae (Sparrows)
Size: 5.5"
Season: Year-round in eastern Virginia; summer in western Virginia
Habitat: Dry fields, woodland edges, gardens

The Chipping Sparrow is a medium-size sparrow with a slightly notched tail and rounded crest. It is barred black and brown on the upperparts, with a gray rump, and is pale gray below. The head has a rufous crown, a white superciliary stripe, dark eye lines, and a white throat. The bill is short, conical, and pointed. Sexes are similar, and winter adults are duller and lack rufous on the crown. Chipping Sparrows feed from trees or open ground in loose flocks, searching for seeds and insects. Voice is a rapid, staccato chipping sound. The breeding adult is illustrated.

Field Sparrow, *Spizella pusilla*
Family Emberizidae (Sparrows)
Size: 5.75"
Season: Year-round
Habitat: Fields with bushy cover or
scattered trees

The Field Sparrow is rather slender and plain colored, with a long, notched tail and a thick-based, stubby, pinkish bill. It is brownish above, with dark streaking and pale wing bars, and grayish below, with a rufous wash along the breast and flanks. The head is mostly gray, with a rufous crown and upper auricular patches and distinct, thin, white eye rings. The sexes are similar; juveniles are duller overall with moderate dark streaking on the breast. Field Sparrows forage on the ground and brush for seeds and insects and sing, often from a conspicuous perch, a series of clear high notes that gradually increase in speed to a rapid trill. The adult is illustrated.

Grasshopper Sparrow,

Ammodramus savannarum
Family Emberizidae (Sparrows)
Size: 5"
Season: Summer
Habitat: Grassland with scrub

The Grasshopper Sparrow has a large, flattened head and a short tail. It is streaked brown, white, and black above and unstreaked buff below. The head is plain buff with a darkish spot on the cheek and dark crown stripes between a light medial stripe. The sexes are similar, while juveniles show noticeable streaking across the breast and flanks. Grasshopper Sparrows feed in grasses or on the ground for grasshoppers (of course!), other insects, and seeds, and may sing from a conspicuous perch a drawn out, thin, buzzy song and short *chip* notes. They often run when alarmed, or fly in erratic, weak spurts. The adult is illustrated.

Saltmarsh Sparrow,
Ammodramus caudacutus
Family Emberizidae (Sparrows)
Size: 5.25"
Season: Year-round
Habitat: Salt- or freshwater marshes, grasslands

The Saltmarsh Sparrow is a ground-dwelling, thick-necked sparrow with a flatish crown. The tail is short with pointed feathers, which is where it gets its name. Plumage is streaked brownish above with contrasting white streaks, while the underside is white and heavily streaked, with an orange wash on the sides. The nape is gray, and the crown and auriculars are dark, surrounded by an orange superciliary stripe, ear patches, and malar area. This bird stays low to the ground, even in flight, and quickly dives for cover. It was once considered conspecific with the Nelson's Sparrow, as the Sharp-tailed Sparrow. The adult is illustrated.

Seaside Sparrow,
Ammodramus maritimus
Family Emberizidae (Sparrows)
Size: 6"
Season: Year-round
Habitat: Coastal saltwater marshes, freshwater marshes

The Seaside Sparrow is plump with a relatively large, flat head; a fairly long bill; and a short tail. Plumage is olive-brown above with dark streaking, and white below with dark streaks or spots. The chin is white, bordered by an obvious moustachial stripe, and the supraloral region is yellow. This bird forages among the marsh vegetation for insects, seeds, and small crustaceans and snails. It dives quickly into cover from flight. The adult is illustrated.

Song Sparrow, *Melospiza melodia*
Family Emberizidae (Sparrows)
Size: 6"
Season: Year-round
Habitat: Thickets, shrubs, woodland edges near water

One of Virginia's most common sparrows, the Song Sparrow is fairly plump with a long, rounded tail. It is brown and gray with streaking above, and white below, with heavy dark streaking that often converges into a discreet spot in the middle of the breast. The head has a dark crown with a gray medial stripe, dark eye lines, and a dark malar stripe above the white chin. Song Sparrows are usually seen in small groups or individually foraging on the ground for insects and seeds. The call is a *chip, chip, chip,* and the song consists of a few clear, deliberate notes followed by a rapid trill. The adult is illustrated.

Summer Tanager, *Piranga rubra*
Family Cardinalidae (Cardinals, Tanagers, Grosbeaks, Buntings)
Size: 7.75"
Season: Summer
Habitat: Mixed pine and oak woodlands

The Summer Tanager lives high in the tree canopy, where it voices a musical song and forages for insects and fruit. It is a relatively large, heavy-billed tanager with a crown that is often peaked in the middle. The male is variable shades of red over the entire body, while the female is olive or brownish yellow above and dull yellow below. Juveniles are similar to the females but have a patchy red head and breast. The adult male is illustrated.

Scarlet Tanager, *Piranga olivacea*
Family Cardinalidae (Cardinals, Tanagers, Grosbeaks, Buntings)
Size: 7"
Season: Summer
Habitat: Leafy deciduous forests, suburban parks

The Scarlet Tanager is a secretive bird of the high canopy that is often detected first by its voice, despite its bright plumage. The breeding male is rich scarlet red overall, with contrasting black wings and tail. Females and nonbreeding males are similar, colored olive-yellow above and yellow below, with dark wings and tail. Males in fall molt show a patchwork of yellow, green, and red feathers. Scarlet Tanagers feed on insects, spiders, and berries at the upper levels of large trees and sing a series of raspy, quick phrases, comparable to that of a robin. The breeding (bottom) and nonbreeding (top) male are illustrated.

Northern Cardinal,
Cardinalis cardinalis
Family Cardinalidae (Cardinals, Tanagers, Grosbeaks, Buntings)
Size: 8.5"
Season: Year-round
Habitat: Woodlands with thickets, suburban gardens

The state bird of Virginia, the Northern Cardinal, with its thick, powerful bill, eats mostly seeds but will also forage for fruit and insects. It is often found in pairs and is quite common at suburban feeders. It is a long-tailed songbird with a thick, short, orange bill and a tall crest. The male is red overall, with a black mask and chin. The female is brownish above and dusky below, crested, and has a dark front to the face. Juveniles are similar to females but have a black bill. The voice is a musical *weeta-weeta* or *woit* heard from a tall, exposed perch. The adult male (bottom) and female (top) are illustrated.

Blue Grosbeak,
Guiraca caerulea
Family Cardinalidae (Cardinals, Tanagers,
Grosbeaks, Buntings)
Size: 6.5"
Season: Summer
Habitat: Woodland edges,
thickets, fields

Grosbeaks get their name from the French word *gros,* which means "large," referring to the birds' massive, conical bills. The male Blue Grosbeak is azure blue overall, with a rufous wing bar and shoulder patch, and black at the front of the face, with a horn-colored bill. The female is brown overall and paler below, with lighter wing bars and lores. The similar Indigo Bunting is smaller, has a smaller bill, and lacks the rufous color on the wings. Blue Grosbeaks eat seeds, fruits, and insects in open areas and habitually flick their tails. They often perch and sing for extended periods with a meandering, warbling song. The adult male (bottom) and female (top) are illustrated.

Indigo Bunting, *Passerina cyanea*
Family Cardinalidae (Cardinals, Tanagers,
Grosbeaks, Buntings)
Size: 5.5"
Season: Summer
Habitat: Brush, open woodlands, fields

Often occurring in large flocks, the Indigo Bunting forages mostly on the ground for insects, berries, and seeds. It is a compact, small songbird with a short, thick bill. The male is entirely blue; the head is a dark, purplish blue, and the body is a lighter sky blue. The female is brownish gray above and duller below, with faint streaking on the breast that meets a white throat. The winter male is smudged with patchy gray, brown, and white. Indigo Buntings perch in treetops, voicing their undulating, chirping melodies. The breeding male (bottom) and female (top) are illustrated.

Red-winged Blackbird,

Agelaius phoeniceus
Family Icteridae (Blackbirds, Grackles, Orioles)
Size: 8.5"
Season: Year-round
Habitat: Marshes, meadows, agricultural areas near water

The Red-winged Blackbird is a widespread, ubiquitous, chunky meadow dweller that forms huge flocks during the nonbreeding season. The male is deep black overall, with bright orange-red lesser coverts and pale median coverts that form an obvious shoulder patch in flight but may be partially concealed on the perched bird. The female is barred tan and dark brown overall, with a pale superciliary stripe and malar patch. Red-winged Blackbirds forage the marshland for insects, spiders, and seeds. The voice is a loud, raspy vibrating *konk-a-leee* given from a perch atop a tall reed or branch. The adult male (bottom) and female (top) are illustrated.

Eastern Meadowlark,

Sturnella magna
Family Icteridae (Blackbirds, Grackles, Orioles)
Size: 9.5"
Season: Year-round
Habitat: Open fields, grasslands, meadows

The Eastern Meadowlark is a chunky, short-tailed icterid with a flat head and a long, pointed bill. It is heavily streaked and barred above and yellow beneath with dark streaking. The head has a dark crown, a white superciliary stripe, dark eye lines, and a yellow chin. On the upper breast is a black V-shaped necklace that becomes quite pale during winter months. Meadowlarks gather in loose flocks to pick through the grass for insects and seeds. They often perch on telephone wires or posts to sing their short whistling phrases. The breeding adult is illustrated.

Rusty Blackbird, *Euphagus carolinus*
Family Icteridae (Blackbirds, Grackles, Orioles)
Size: 9"
Season: Winter
Habitat: Marshes, riversides, pastures near water

The Rusty Blackbird is a sleek, medium-size blackbird that resembles the Brewer's Blackbird, whose range is farther west. The breeding male is matte black overall, with contrasting pale yellow eyes. The winter male is dark but barred with rusty brown along the back and breast and has a mostly brown head except for the lores and auricular area. The winter female is paler still, with lighter brown above and on the head, and has a grayish rump. Rusty Blackbirds feed in small flocks in shallow water for aquatic invertebrates or in nearby fields for seeds. Song is a series of chattery, squeaky, jumbled notes accented at the end with a louder, high-pitched *ee*. Once quite abundant, the Rusty Blackbird's numbers have decreased dramatically in recent years. The breeding male (bottom) and female (top) are illustrated.

Common Grackle,
Quiscalus quiscula
Family Icteridae (Blackbirds, Grackles, Orioles)
Size: 12.5"
Season: Year-round
Habitat: Pastures, open woodlands, urban parks

The Common Grackle is a large blackbird but smaller than the Boat-tailed Grackle. The body is elongated with a long, heavy bill and long tail, which is fatter toward the tip and often folded into a keel shape. Plumage is overall black with a metallic sheen of purple on the head and brown on the wings and underside. The eyes are a contrasting light yellow color. Quite social, Common Grackles form huge flocks with other blackbirds and forage on the ground for just about any kind of food, including insects, grains, refuse, and crustaceans. Voice is a high-pitched, rasping trill. The adult male is illustrated.

Boat-tailed Grackle,
Quiscalus major
Family Icteridae (Blackbirds, Grackles, Orioles)
Size: 14–16"; males larger than females
Season: Year-round
Habitat: Salt- or freshwater marshes near the coast

The Boat-tailed Grackle is larger than the Common Grackle and less likely to form large flocks. It has long legs and a long, broad, spatula-shaped tail that is often folded in a keel shape. The male is black overall, with a metallic, blue-green sheen over the head and body. The female is smaller with a shorter tail, is brownish overall, and has a lighter head with dark striping along the eye lines, under the crown, and along the malar area. The eyes of northern birds are light yellow, while those farther south have darker, brown eyes. Boat-tailed Grackles pick the ground for insects, seeds, and crustaceans. The adult male (bottom) and female (top) are illustrated.

Brown-headed Cowbird, *Molothrus ater*
Family Icteridae (Blackbirds, Grackles, Orioles)
Size: 7.5"
Season: Year-round
Habitat: Woodland edges, pastures with livestock, grassy fields

The Brown-headed Cowbird is a stocky, short-winged, and short-tailed blackbird with a short, conical bill. The male is glossy black overall with a chocolate-brown head. The female is light brown overall, with faint streaking on the underparts and a pale throat. Cowbirds often feed in flocks with other blackbirds, picking out seeds and insects from the ground. Voice is a number of gurgling, squeaking phrases. Cowbirds practice brood parasitism; they lay their eggs in the nests of other passerine species that then raise their young. Hence, their presence often reduces the populations of other songbirds. The adult male is illustrated.

Orchard Oriole, *Icterus spurius*
Family Icteridae (Blackbirds, Grackles, Orioles)
Size: 7"
Season: Summer
Habitat: Orchards, open woodlands, parks

The Orchard Oriole is a small oriole with a relatively thin, short bill and a short tail that it often tilts sideways. The male is black above with a red rump and a black, hooded head. The underside is reddish or orange-brown with a similarly colored shoulder patch. The lower mandible is light blue-gray. Females are markedly different; they are greenish gray above and bright yellow below, with two white wing bars. Juveniles are similar to females but have black chins and lores. Orchard Orioles feed in trees for insects, fruit, and nectar and emit high, erratic musical whistles and chirps. The adult male (bottom) and female (top) are illustrated.

Baltimore Oriole, *Icterus galbula*
Family Icteridae (Blackbirds, Grackles, Orioles)
Size: 8.5"
Season: Summer
Habitat: Deciduous woodlands, suburban gardens, parks

The Baltimore Oriole is a somewhat stocky icterid with a short, squared tail and a straight, tapered bill. The male is bright yellow-orange with a black hood. Wings are black with white edging the flight feathers and coverts, and there is a yellow-orange shoulder patch. The tail is orange with black along the base and down the middle. The female is paler along the sides, with a white shoulder patch and a mottled, yellow and brown head and plain tail. The Baltimore Oriole forages for insects, fruits, and nectar from the leafy canopy. It is sometimes considered, with Bullock's Oriole, as one species, the Northern Oriole. The adult male (bottom) and female (top) are illustrated.

House Finch, *Carpodacus mexicanus*
Family Fringillidae (Finches)
Size: 6"
Season: Year-round
Habitat: Woodland edges, urban areas

The House Finch is a western species that has been introduced to eastern North America and is now common and widespread in Virginia, especially in urban areas. A relatively slim finch, it has a longish, slightly notched tail and a short, conical bill with a down-curved culmen. The male is brown above, with streaking on the back, and pale below with heavy streaking. An orange-red wash pervades the supercilium, throat, and upper breast. The female is a drab gray-brown with similar streaking on the back and underside, with no red on the face or breast. House Finches have a variable diet that includes seeds, insects, and fruits, and they are often the most abundant bird visiting feeders. Voice is a rapid musical warble. The adult male is illustrated.

American Goldfinch,

Spinus tristis
Family Fringillidae (Finches)
Size: 5"
Season: Year-round
Habitat: Open fields, marshes, urban feeders

The American Goldfinch is a small, cheerful, social finch with a short, notched tail and a small, conical bill. In winter it is brownish gray, lighter underneath, with black wings and tail. There is bright yellow on the shoulder, around the eyes, and along the chin, and there are two white wing bars. In breeding plumage, the male becomes light yellow arcross the back, undersides, and head and develops a black forehead and loral area. Also, the bill becomes orange. Females are similar to winter males. American Goldfinches forage by actively searching for insects and seeds of all kinds, particularly thistle. Voice is a meandering musical warble, including high *cheep* notes. The breeding (bottom) and nonbreeding (top) male are illustrated.

FINCHES

House Sparrow,

Passer domesticus
Family Passeridae (Old World Sparrows)
Size: 6.25"
Season: Year-round
Habitat: Urban environments, rural pastures

Introduced from Europe, the House Sparrow is ubiquitous in almost every city in the United States and is often the only sparrow-type bird seen in urban areas. It is stocky, aggressive, and gregarious and has a relatively large head and short, finch-like bill. Males are streaked brown and black above and pale below. The lores, chin, and breast are black, while the crown and auriculars are gray. There is a prominent white wing bar at the median coverts. In winter the male lacks the dark breast patch. Females are drab overall with a lighter bill and pale supercilium. House Sparrows have a highly varied diet, including grains, insects, berries, and crumbs from local cafes. Voice is a series of rather unmusical chirps. The breeding male (bottom) and a female (top) are illustrated.

Index

About the Author/Illustrator

Todd Telander is a naturalist illustrator/artist living in Walla Walla, Washington. He has studied and illustrated wildlife since 1988 while living in California, Colorado, New Mexico, and Washington. He graduated from the University of California at Santa Cruz with degrees in biology, environmental studies, and scientific illustration and has since illustrated numerous books and other publications. His wife, Kirsten Telander, is a  writer; they have two boys, Miles and Oliver. Todd's work can be viewed online at toddtelander.com.